HERMENEUTICS AND UNIFICATION THEOLOGY

Edited by
Darrol Bryant
Durwood Foster

Distributed by
The Rose of Sharon Press, Inc.
New York

Conference Series no. 5
First edition
© 1980
by

The Unification Theological Seminary
Barrytown, New York 12507

Distributed by
The Rose of Sharon Press, Inc.
G.P.O. Box 2432
New York, N.Y. 10001

Printed in the United States of America
Library of Congress Cataloging number 80-66201
ISBN 0-932894-05-4

CONTENTS

PREFACE

The present volume grew out of a theological conversation held in Berkeley, California, in the spring of 1979. The participants were theological students from the Unification Church, theologians of several Christian traditions, and professional scholars in the field of religion. The conference was sponsored by the Unification Theological Seminary, Barrytown, New York, as part of its on-going conference program.

Over the past three years the Unification Theological Seminary has sponsored more than twenty such conferences. Each of these meetings has brought together participants from a wide range of Christian traditions, theological commitments and scholarly disciplines. Each of these meetings has had its own distinctive character, a distinctiveness rooted in the composition of the group, the questions that are raised and pursued and the dynamic which emerges as the conversation unfolds. From these meetings two previous volumes have appeared: *Exploring Unification Theology* (1978) and *Evangelical-Unification Dialogue* (1979).

Like the earlier volumes, this volume documents a certain moment in the evolution of these theological conversations. Here we find the record of a theological conversation of considerable depth that, in large measure, focused on an issue. The issue is hermeneutics. In broad strokes the issue here is two-fold. First, how are we to read or interpret the Unification movement? What understandings of the cultural context and historical moment in which this movement emerged are required for us, as theologians and students of religion, to rightly interpret what the movement is about? Do the philosophical assumptions and cultural patterns of the East stamp the Unification movement in a distinctive way? What are the points of convergence and divergence that we, trained in the theological and religious disciplines of the West have to become aware of to read this movement aright? Secondly, what are the hermeneutical principles which shape and guide the Unification articulation of theology in its reading of the Christian scriptures? What are the operative principles and questions — philosophical, cultural and theological — which lie at the center of the theology of the Unification movement? Why does it read the story of creation in the way it does? or the fall? or redemption? or eschatology? How does the interpretation of Christian doctrine that we find in the *Divine Principle* relate to the long traditions of theological reflection we know in the West?

Obviously, these questions double back on one another. More importantly, these issues are, in this conversation, more raised and explored than they are resolved. As in any good conversation, we found ourselves running up against the limits of our varied competencies and knowledge. Time and again we found ourselves wishing we had other people involved in the conversation. At the same time, it is precisely the combination of moments of insight and ignorance that make this a document worth sharing with a larger community.

As indicated above, the present volume is the third to have emerged from the theological conversations that have taken place over the past three years. It is perhaps worth considering this present document in the light of the longer history of conversation and publication. When viewed in relation to the two earlier volumes, this volume testifies to a discernible evolution in the history of these meetings. The first meetings were necessarily more expository in nature since the participants were largely uninformed about the Unification movement. This stage of exposition and critique is reflected in *Exploring Unification Theology*. At a second stage, reflected in *Evangelical-Unification Dialogue,* the conversation moved from exposition to exchange. But here the dialogue was characterized by overagainstness since the participants represented a strand of Evangelical theology highly sensitive to doctrinal differences with Unification theology. With the publication of the present volume one can see yet another stage beginning to emerge: the exploration of an issue which, while focused on the Unification movement, is of larger theological import. In this conversation the participants were grappling with issues that are at the very center of contemporary theological debate. How are we to speak of God and the human condition? What light does theology throw on the human situation? What are the sources of authority in theology? How is Scripture to be read? Does theology need drastic recasting? What is the meaning of ecumenical Christianity when we move beyond the boundaries of the West?

While the purposes of the Unification Theological Seminary in the sponsorship of these meetings are openly apologetic (they believe that exposure to their students will result in a more fair-minded reading of the movement than has been received at the hands of the popular press) and educational (they believe that these conferences are crucial to the education of their own students), they are also theological. The theological purpose grows out of the conviction within the Unification movement that we need to find settings for the doing of theology that move beyond the divisions that still, far too much, characterize theology in the West. Mr. David Kim, president of the Seminary, affirms in this conversation his commitment to ecumenical theology, which is also reflected in the ecumenical composition of the faculty at the Seminary. It is in order to move in the direction of a more ecumenical theology that the Seminary has taken upon itself the task of sponsoring meetings where theologians not only meet members of the Unification Church, but each other as well. For some of the participants in these meetings these are the first occasions they have had to engage in significant theological conversation with people from traditions other than their own. Catholics, Presbyterians, Lutherans, Evangelicals, Methodists, Baptists, Jehovah's Witnesses and many others have met in these settings. While the ecumenical commitments of the Unification movement are certainly not unique, they are worth noting in order that we better grasp the background and motivation for this conversation in Berkeley as a part of an ongoing commitment of the Seminary to contemporary theological reflection.

What we may see emerging in these conferences is a new context and setting for theological discussion and articulation. Thus, in a sense, the form of these meetings may well prove to be as significant as their content. In these contexts we are all challenged to articulate our theologies in a context of multiplicity and direct exchange constantly aware that other theological options are living commitments held by others present in the discussion. Here there is generated a dynamic that transforms our consciousness of the theological project, or at least impinges upon that project, in the very process of theological articulation. Here one cannot presuppose like-mindedness as the common ground of conversation but one must acknowledge our "distemporaniety" (Rosenstock-Huessy) in order to create the necessary "contemporaniety" for a shared theological vocation.

The sharing of personal stories is crucial to the generation of the "contemporaniety" requisite for the conversation. As the reader will notice, the participants are thus disclosed to one another as persons engaged in their unique way by life's varied claims, rather than as religious, vocational or theological abstractions. Through the sharing of personal stories a certain depth, as well as a subtext, is given to the conversation. In this process each of the participants has some access to the personal stories that shape each of us as we approach the larger task of theological articulation. This feature of the conversation is not, we believe, incidental to what happens but integral. Consequently, the present volume has retained these personal stories as they were given there.

While this volume documents a conversation on a theme of considerable contemporary theological interest, it does not arrive at any conclusions. Rather, it is a record of a conversation. And, like any conversation, it has its lacunae and lapses; it is open-ended. Indeed, the last section of the text—the conversation with Dr. Mose Durst—is really a conversation linked to the preceeding sections only by proximity in time. We have, nonetheless, retained it in the present volume because we believe it may prove of interest to students of the Unification movement. Moreover, it testifies to another aspect of these meetings, namely, the intra-Unification discussion between different parts of the movement. As indicated in the text, many of the allegations leveled against the Unification Church center around the Bay Area community. Thus it seemed desirable to include that conversation, as it were, for the record.

The transcripts of our meeting were edited and are here presented in the order in which the conversation occurred. We have asked all the participants to read the edited version and they have graciously assented to our edited account of what they said. As with the earlier volumes, the editorial principle we have subscribed to throughout is that of intelligibility. We trust that the result of our efforts will prove of interest to those who, either professionally or religiously, are concerned to understand something more of this admittedly controversial religious movement. Also, because of the controversy surrounding the movement, one of the participants has decided to take on a pseudonym.

As those of us who participated in this conversation came to see and as is evident in the text, the Unification movement is both continuous and discontinuous with other Christian traditions that we know. Regardless of our evaluation of the merits or demerits of the specific theological claims that are emerging in the Unification movement, we would hope that our readers will share something of our conviction that in the young theologians of the Unification movement we have some impressive new voices in the larger theological conversation.

Finally, we wish to thank Barbara Mallory, Karen Miller and Yolanda Smalls who transcribed the tapes, Sylvia Grahn and Sara Witt for help in proofreading, and John Maniatis and Lynn Musgrave who with consistent good humor and patience have seen the manuscript through to publication.

January 16, 1980   D.F.

                                                         M.D.B.

PARTICIPANTS

Dagfinn Aslid, graduate of Unification Theological Seminary and student, School of Theology at Claremont, Claremont, Ca.

George Baker, Program for the Study of New Religious Movements, Graduate Theological Union, Berkeley, Ca.

M. Darrol Bryant, Associate Professor of Religion and Culture, Renison College, University of Waterloo, Waterloo, Ontario.

Linda Duddy, researcher, writer, Berkeley, Ca.

Neil Duddy, researcher, writer, Berkeley, Ca.

Mose Durst, director of the Unification Church in Northern California.

Durwood Foster, Professor of Systematic Theology, Pacific School of Religion, Berkeley, Ca.

Anthony Guerra, graduate of Unification Theological Seminary and student, Harvard Divinity School, Cambridge, Ma.

Virginia Hearn, editor, writer, Berkeley, Ca.

Walter Hearn, editor, writer, Berkeley, Ca.

J. Stillson Judah, Emeritus Professor of History of Religions, Pacific School of Religion and Librarian Emeritus, Graduate Theological Union, Berkeley, Ca.

Mark Juergensmeyer, Professor of Ethics and Phenomenology of Religion, Graduate Theological Union and University of California, Berkeley, Ca.

David Kim, President of Unification Theological Seminary, Barrytown, N.Y.

Yoshihiko Masuda, graduate of Unification Theological Seminary and student, Graduate Theological Union, Berkeley, Ca.

Michael Mickler, graduate of Unification Theological Seminary and student, Graduate Theological Union, Berkeley, Ca.

Matthew Morrison, member of the Unification Church, Oakland, Ca.

Richard Quebedeaux, author, Berkeley, Ca.

Lewis Rambo, Assistant Professor of Pastoral Psychology, San Francisco Theological Seminary, San Anselmo, Ca.

Herbert Richardson, Professor of Theology, St. Michael's College, University of Toronto, Toronto, Ontario

Holly Sherman, student, Unification Theological Seminary, Barrytown, N.Y.

Theologian X

Jonathan Wells, graduate of Unification Theological Seminary and student, Yale University, New Haven, Ct.

Patricia Zulkosky, graduate of Unification Theological Seminary and student, School of Theology at Claremont, Claremont, Ca.

A cross section of participants at the conference. From left to right: Richard Quebedeaux, J. Stillson Judah, Walter Hearn, Virginia Hearn, Yoshihiko Masuda, Mose Durst. Those in the foreground with only their backs visible have not been identified.

Getting Acquainted: the Hermeneutics of Personal Story

Darrol Bryant: We want to begin this evening by giving people a chance to introduce themselves. I'll begin by telling a little bit of my story. I teach in the area of religion and culture at Renison College, the University of Waterloo, in Waterloo, Ontario, Canada. I'm originally from North Dakota where I grew up in a small town right next to the Canadian border. I went to Concordia College in Moorehead, Minnesota, a Lutheran school, where I studied philosophy and political science. Then I studied theology at Harvard Divinity School. In 1967 I went to Waterloo for the first time, where I taught at Waterloo Lutheran University for a couple of years. Then I spent a year with the Lutheran World Federation in Geneva, organizing a conference for young Lutherans from around the world. So I guess I've been in the business of organizing conferences for more than a decade. I returned to Canada to study with Dr. Richardson, who had been a teacher of mine before and had since moved to St. Michael's College at the University of Toronto. And that was the unlikely setting where I began studying Jonathan Edwards. It was an interesting time to be outside of America, in a Catholic milieu, studying America's greatest Protestant theologian.

Three years ago I went to the Unification Theological Seminary at Barrytown. I went with considerable misgiving, but was intrigued by what I found. Given my background in American religion, I read the movement in the light of the millennial movements and eschatological themes that have characterized American religious life through its history. At the time I went to Barrytown, I was just getting to the point where I was seeing

Edward's millennialism as an unfortunate aspect of his theology. Then I found myself confronted again with a group that had a strong sense of living in a critical juncture in the history of the human race. All of Edward's great speeches about the dawning of the millennium here in America started to come back and haunt me again. I've spent the last three years reassessing that aspect of Edward's life and thought. This is especially problematical to me as a Lutheran. We Lutherans tend not to have a very strong doctrine, or any doctrine whatsoever, of eschatology. Lutheran theology tends to be centered fundamentally and totally on the doctrine of redemption. Consequently, the encounter with the Unification movement has led to an interesting process of re-evaluation of my own theological heritage in conversation with a group of people who are centered in eschatological doctrine. That is the background that brings me to this conversation.

I'm here because I like the opportunity to orchestrate conversations, and to see the multiplicity of positions that get articulated, both from the various people who come to these conferences and the members of the Unification Church itself. You could say that I'm a moderator in search of the theology of the Unification Church. Once I get that nailed down, then perhaps I can be very clear about the content of these meetings. As it is, it seems, as I said to Stillson Judah, that every time we meet we have a very different conference because different people come and raise different questions, and in response to those questions the theology looks each time a little different.

Dagfinn Aslid: My name is Dagfinn Aslid. It's a Norwegian name. I was born in a picture postcard setting in western Norway where I grew up in a community which was very Christian. In my home town you might say we breathed Christianity—it was just part of the life of the village. So I guess I could say I grew up Christian without knowing myself otherwise in a little fjord in western Norway. I left home for the first time when I was 18 to go to America in Wisconsin on an American Field Service scholarship. I ended up at Wisconsin Lutheran High School, a school of the Wisconsin Synod. So that started me thinking about what I believed. Then I went back to Norway and finished military service on the Russian border. After that I went to Paris for my studies at the Sorbonne where I enrolled in 1968 in psychology. At that time students weren't studying, they were throwing bricks. It was the time of the student revolution there. Police were chasing anybody they could find and I ended up going to Alaska. (laughter) There I fished for king crab and got rich, and bought a Harley-Davidson which I rode across America. I went back to Paris in 1969. I found that the whole university system had been turned upside down. In 1970 I was offered a job with a Norwegian radio station where I worked for a year as a reporter. From then on for about four years I traveled between Paris where I went to school, my home, and America where I went fishing. Later I lived in Paris earning my living playing Dixieland jazz.

It was in Sweden in 1974 that I first met the Unification Church on the street. I heard a little voice asking me if I was interested in philosophy and religion, and I thought, "Oh, no, not one of those sects." But it turned out to be a very wise Moonie who could do a lot of listening as well as asking questions. At that time there were five members in the whole of Sweden. It was a different situation from what you see in America now. It was a small group of very idealistic people and that appealed to me. I was very moved by these people and their burning idealism. I had to locate for myself something meaningful to dedicate my life to, and what I found was something that not only had a lot of enthusiasm involved in it but also had an intellectual openness. Those two things together persuaded me to start working in Sweden. In 1976 I came to America and went to the Seminary in Barrytown, and graduated in 1978. Now I am at Claremont School of Theology and am finishing my Master's there, and then I'm going to the program at Claremont Graduate School in philosophy of religion and theology.

Lewis Rambo: My name is Lewis Rambo, I grew up in Comanche, Texas. If you ever saw the movie "The Last Picture Show," that will give you some idea of what it was like where I grew up. I went to Abilene Christian College in Abilene, Texas, served a year as minister of a Church of Christ in Reading, Pennsylvania, then went to Yale Divinity School for three years, and to the University of Chicago for a Ph.D. I taught at Trinity College, just outside of Chicago, for three years in the Psychology Department. In September, I moved to San Francisco Theological Seminary and the Graduate Theological Union (GTU) to teach psychology of religion and pastoral psychology. My interest is the conversion process.

Mark Juergensmeyer: I'm Mark Juergensmeyer, and I teach at the University of California at Berkeley, where I co-ordinate the Religious Studies Program, and at the Graduate Theological Union where I'm involved in the history of religions. I'm a Methodist by background. I come from southern Illinois, from a town every bit as boring as Comanche, Texas. I went to Union Theological Seminary where I worked with Reinhold Niebuhr, did graduate work in religion and society, and then spent a number of years in India. I just finished a book on religion and the untouchables. I'm interested in modern religions in India and I'm also interested in ethics. I'll be back in India this summer working on a book on the modern religious movements in that country.

Mike Mickler: And you were a teen-age evangelist.

Mark Juergensmeyer: Now, Mike, come off it. Mike was in the seminar I taught on the social scientific study of religious movements; and Jonathan and I discovered we knew each other· 10 years ago when Jonathan was not in the Unification Church, but was something of a celebrity in the anti-war movement.

David Kim: My name is David Kim. At the dinner table Dr. Bryant already introduced me. I'm administratively in charge of Barrytown, but not theologically. My concern all the time is how to expand ecumenism. I like to call Barrytown "Ecumenism Seminary." I have that kind of a dream. Before I met Rev. Moon, I had a concept of "United Religions" similar to the United Nations structure. When I first met Rev. Moon in 1954, he already had the idea of the "Unification of Religions." I am really working hard to find the common ecumenical grounds through which we Christians can work together. Recently Dr. Lewis of our Seminary has been developing a project called "The Global Congress of World Religions." So far seven or eight private groups plan to work together and to sponsor the "Global Congress" project.

I hope you won't be influenced by my presence here. Actually, I'd like to be here as an observer, not to talk too much, but to learn something. Sometimes you people like to ask crucial questions directly to a close friend of Rev. Moon, and it is natural. But this is a theological dialogue between our seminary students and other participants. Therefore, instead of me talking too much, I'd like to remain as an observer as much as possible. Thank you.

Herbert Richardson: I'm Herb Richardson, and I'm a systematic theologian. I'm Presbyterian by denomination and Roman Catholic by sensibility and spirituality. I pray not only to Jesus but also to the Virgin Mary.

My family was displaced at the time of the Depression from Massachusetts to Ohio. My grandmother's name was Mary Margara McGwynn, from Ireland. The Richardsons represent the New England and Calvinist side of my character. My grandmother represents the Irish and Virgin Mary heritage.

My immediate family was non-religious. My father thought religion was good for comforting old ladies. My mother and I were not allowed to go to Sunday school. A couple of times, I protested and attended secretly. When I was 19, my father became very ill and almost died, and I started thinking about religious questions. On the basis of that reflection, I joined a local Presbyterian church. I had not read Calvin or any books on Presbyterianism. I had not undergone any kind of conversion in the evangelical sense. But there was some kind of inward commitment there.

Over the next few years, I got myself located theologically. By the mid-fifties, I was a real Calvinist, which I remain today. I got my Ph.D. at Harvard, studied in both France and Germany, and was invited back to Harvard to start teaching. That was in 1962. One of the most important spiritual experiences of my life was that Harvard held a large Roman Catholic-Protestant Colloquium in the spring of 1963 and I went to it. This meeting and close work with good Catholic theologians forced me to rethink everything. (My childhood view of Catholics came from my growing up in a Catholic ethnic ghetto, where we non-Catholics were a minority. The gossip was that we were free kids who went to public schools, while the Catholic kids went to superstitious parochial schools. The gossip was that their priests did dirty sexual things with nuns, and that the Catholic Church was controlled by a foreign power and it was a financial rip-off. When you met nice Catholic people, you had to explain that in your theory. So then we said, "Well, they're not very Catholic.")

For the next six years at Harvard I taught all the courses in Catholic Theology. The college told me, "You can have the whole field." I taught St. Augustine, St. Anselm, St. Thomas, Authority and Tradition and other such stuff. As this went on I became more and more interested in Catholic theology and I also became more eager for the Harvard faculty to appoint a Catholic. Whenever we would look for a Catholic to be on the faculty, it always turned out that somehow they were not really "qualified." I thought this to be a bunch of nonsense. So I said to myself, "If you want some Catholic colleagues, why don't you go get them?"

So I went to teach in a Catholic faculty, St. Michael's College in Toronto. At that time Bernard Lonergan, Gregory Baum, and Leslie Dewart were there. It was a very good Catholic faculty. When I went up to St. Michael's, the reaction of some of my Protestant colleagues was that I was out of my mind and had sold out. They said, "You're ruining your theological career. Nobody will take you seriously any more. Don't do it." They actually asked me, "Do you really have the freedom to teach what you want in the classroom?" When in the mid-seventies I taught a course at the Unification Theological Seminary, I heard all the same things again — this time against Moonies rather than Catholics.

All of the things that had been told to me about the Catholics when I was growing up, I was now hearing about the Moonies: that the Moonies are controlled by a foreign power; that they're really more interested in money than in religious things; that their thinking is not free. (In my youth we didn't call it brainwashing, but superstition. Then, we wanted to get the Catholic kids out of parochial schools so that they could make up their own minds.)

I want to say three more things and then I'll stop: I came from a secular family. I mentioned my father's illness that was at the time that I joined the Christian church. However, another positive factor was the influence and teaching of Jim Lawson, who was one of Martin Luther King's closest friends. Thus, my initial Christian commitment in a way was to King and what he stood for. For 10 years of my life Martin Luther King was Jesus Christ to me. I always felt that through the power of this man's life, I best understood who Jesus Christ was. I believe we must overcome racism, so I feel solidarity with the Unification Church's practice of creating interracial marriages.

The second thing that has attracted me to the Unification Church was my belief in Christian missions. When I was in India, I saw that the world has only two options: Marxism or Christianity. I'm with Unification Church partly because of its profound commitment to missions. This means not just converting people to Jesus Christ, but also building a unified world.

The third thing that attracts me to the Unification movement is that I believe that Jesus Christ brings new and transformed life. I believe the church must preach not just the forgiveness of sins, but also new life and transformed character. I'm a perfectionist. This means I believe that to establish the Kingdom of God on earth, there has to be not merely a better social structure but also better people. Part of the way that better people are formed is through the work of Jesus Christ in the soul, and the task of the church is to bring this to pass.

It's because I see the Unification movement struggling to fight racism, to support missions, and to create better people that I identify with it. I don't have any particular beliefs about Rev. Moon. It's more the Unification movement and theology that I like. But I don't have any problems with Rev. Moon either. At the Unification Seminary, I had a chance to speak with Rev. Moon, so I said, "Rev. Moon, are you the messiah?"

He replied, "Dr. Richardson, I'm going to answer your question. But first we have to know what the messiah is. The messiah is someone who strives with all of his heart, his soul, his mind, his will, to build the Kingdom of God on earth, to do the will of God on earth. *I try to be the messiah; you should try to be the messiah too; we should all try to be the messiah.*"

As he said this I thought, "I see. This is the Old Testament concept of messiah as a community of righteous people."

The idea that God wants us all to be messiahs, that is "Christ to our neighbors" is part of the Christian tradition. For example, Luther said it. So, I don't see the Unification Church as a new religion, rather, I see it as a renewal movement within the church.

Durwood Foster: My name is Durwood Foster. I'm Dean at the Pacific School of Religion here in Berkeley where I also teach systematic theology. I'm amazed at how our various pathways cross and double back upon themselves. I think it was a decade ago that here in this hotel for the first time I encountered the Rev. Moon. Korean friends had asked me to come along with them to hear his presentation. I had seen, just a few days before that, an article in *Time* magazine about the visit to America of this new messianic figure from Korea who claimed to be the Messiah returned. So I came along and heard the address that night interpreted by Col. Pak. I was very fascinated and impressed. On that occasion the Rev. Moon did not settle or even discuss the question of whether he was the Messiah, but he did announce he was launching a campaign to recapture America for God. He was sending out thousands of young people to go across the country in that mission. I was impressed by the enthusiasm of the young people I saw here on that occasion. I wonder where they all are now.

I am from near Plains, Georgia, some 40 miles from the home of Jimmy Carter. It's become a kind of picture post-card since 1972, but a rather different one from Dagfinn's. I was reared in that part of the Bible Belt. Like some of you, Herb, at least, I came from a non-religious home. My parents were not affiliated with a church at all. But somehow I was converted—so I had something to do with conversion from an early age—to the born-again type of evangelical Christianity of the Deep South. And I still have some of that in me, though as I went on from there to the Navy, and then to Emory University and took up the study of psychology and philosophy, I wandered far from my evangelical experience, or at least from the frame of reference that had gone with it.

Feeling the need to get myself together spiritually, I went next to Union Seminary in New York. Reinhold Niebuhr and Paul Tillich especially, and some others also, helped me to put together a new theological perspective. I continued my studies after the M. Div. at Union by going abroad to Heidelberg, so my path crossed with Mr. X's at that point. Then I came back and finished the doctorate in New York at Union and Columbia. I taught for a couple of years at Union after that, then went to Duke, where George Baker was, for awhile. At Duke, I taught in the field of history and phenomenology of religion, which cultivated in me an interest that had not been activated hitherto, and I think it laid the groundwork for some of my response to the new religious movements, the Unification Church as well as a lot of others. It certainly laid the groundwork for my affinity with Stillson Judah who was teaching in that field when I came to Berkeley to teach systematic theology. It led us eventually to take a trip together to India. He was writing a book on Hare Krishna, and I was pursuing the theme of inter-religious dialogue, which I have been for the last decade or so increasingly interested in. I've taken part in a number of dialogues, including the one that finally crystallized into the GTU. Through conversations among faculties that at one time were much more scattered, we decided some 15 years ago there was no good reason why we shouldn't begin merging our teaching programs.

I have many interests that have already been mentioned,

and am not going to recapitulate all of them. Herb states extremely well some of the reasons why I find the Unification movement arresting, challenging, and constantly interesting. I came out of a sort of evangelical experience, as I've indicated, where one wants redemption. But partly because I joined the Methodist Church eventually and, theologically, because I got involved in the theology of Albrecht Ritschl, the theme of the Kingdom of God, the reign of God, became extremely important in my thinking. In my personal perspective and faith and commitment, I think of myself as living and working in and for the Kingdom of God, so there is an eschatological dimension. It's not primarily, or exclusively, an other-worldly kind of eschatology. But it does mean that I feel an alliance with any kind of movement that is working towards the creation of the unification of the human race, that is working to bring down the walls of hostility. For me the normative symbolization of this is the Christ, but I see any energies and efforts and commitments that are working towards this end as being in deep affinity with my own spirit and interest. That provides a bridge—at least I've always felt this, sincerely—with members of the Unification Church whom I've met, people like Mike Mickler and a lot of others.

Stillson Judah: I'm Stillson Judah. I'm Professor Emeritus at the GTU, and presently also at Pacific School of Religion. My main field is history of religions. I started my career in seminaries as a librarian at the Pacific School of Religion. I then eventually became librarian at the GTU. The job there involved trying to put together the nine libraries. I also became professor of history of religions at the GTU, until I retired.

My whole interest in the history of religions parallels in some ways my whole interest in all of the new religious movements. When I was about 12 years old, I was going to a Methodist Sunday school. I didn't find satisfaction there. I told my parents this, and they said I would have to have some type of religious training, and so, I found through an ad in the papers the following Sunday some lectures on Theosophy. I wanted to attend them and my parents took me. This introduced me to the whole theosophical library in Seattle, Washington, which was a library of works on all of the great religions of the world. I became interested then not only in Theosophy, but in the broader aspects of the whole study of world religions. I then began to gravitate into one group after another. I attended the TM Movement for a while, I dabbled a little bit in spiritualism, I sat under various Yogis for several years at a time, spent a summer with Krishnamurti over on Bainbridge Island, and thoroughly involved myself with the whole field of the history of religions. I had no problem, of course, as far as my parents were concerned, because I took them right along with me wherever I was investigating. However, when I was midway along in my undergraduate courses in Oriental Studies at the University of Washington, I came under the influence of Dr. Herbert Henry Gown, professor of oriental studies at the University, who was also an Episcopalian priest. Through his teaching, which I enjoyed very much, I gradually swung back to Christianity. Eventually, you might say, I was reconverted back to Christianity. I became a member of the University Christian Church in Seattle, Washington, primarily because the neighbors had great admiration for the minister. I can't say that it was a spiritual conversion, it was rather an intellectual one. Yet I've always had a great deal of interest in and certainly feel the great importance of what I would consider a genuine spiritual conversion.

My graduate work was largely in the field of Hinduism, Buddhism, and particularly in the languages that these religions involve. I had six years of Sanskrit in my studies of Hinduism and Buddhism. Then when I came to the Pacific School of Religion, after becoming librarian there in 1955, I also became professor of the history of religions. I began to teach in the field, but still I had this great interest in all of these new religions. So in 1957 I began my first serious research while on a sabbatical leave with a Rockefeller grant to study the metaphysical movements in America. This eventually came out in book form 10 years later as *The History and Philosophy of the Metaphysical Movements in America.** It dealt with all of these movements that I had been so much involved in.

Then when the sixties came along I became interested in counter-cultural religions. Durwood Foster first got me interested in the Hare Krishna movement. I was invited to attend a conference back at Princeton University on new religious movements, and I was thinking, what should I really work on. We were going to lunch and we saw these young men dancing and chanting outside

---

*J. Stillson Judah, *The History and Philosophy of the Metaphysical Movements in America*, Philadelphia, Pa.: Westminster Press, 1967.

of Sproul Plaza. He said, "Well, why don't you do a study of the Hare Krishna movement?" I said, "Now that's a good idea." I immediately started an investigation there—participant observation—and I worked out a questionnaire with a sociologist who was a member of the Hare Krishna movement who was also doing graduate work for her Ph.D. under Charles Glock at the University. We worked out very carefully this five page questionnaire so it would be acceptable to the sociologist. We tried to work this out so that we would have all of the counter-cultural aspects that I wanted to bring out in the questionnaire. That became the basis for a sociological and religious study of the Krishna movement.

The next thing I became interested in was the Unification Church. Back in 1962 I met Miss Kim* when she was out here doing her first missionary work in the Bay Area. It was quite interesting. She came up to the library one time, and we became acquainted, and she brought out this long tape. I listened to three hours of this tape on Rev. Moon and the whole movement. Of course, it wasn't called the Unification Church at that time as I recall. It was very strange sounding to me because here was this Korean who was considered the Lord of the Second Advent. At that time, I wasn't very interested in the Unification Church because it didn't seem to be doing anything. There was no great interest in the community. Certainly at that time it was rather small. But it was in the later sixties that it began to really move. I became interested then, because of a friendship with David Hose who was one of the leaders in the church here. He asked me why I didn't write a book on the Unification Church, as I had on the Hare Krishna movement?** Having gotten the proper credentials from President Salonen*** so that I could visit the various centers, I made a national survey of the Unification Church. I visited 16 centers all over the United States, and did hundreds of hours of interviews in addition to getting the statistical information.

I was particularly interested at that time to try to do a work

---

*Miss Young Oon Kim was the first missionary of the Unification Church to come to America. She came to the United States in 1959.

**J. Stillson Judah, *Hare Krishna and the Counterculture*, New York, N.Y.: John Wiley & Sons, 1974.

***Mr. Neil Albert Salonen is president of the Unification Church of America.

like the book I'd written on the Hare Krishna movement, but I wanted to broaden it out. I wanted to include the same type of material for the Unification Church as I had for the Hare Krishna movement, so that I might have a basis of comparison. I also wanted to include a broader aspect, you might say a look into the psychological aspects of the whole movement. So we added a whole extra page of questions on what would be of interest to psychologists. Then, very interestingly, this whole controversy concerning mind control and religious conversion came up. Well, I looked at my data. I had at this time 158 single-spaced pages of just plain data from the questionnaire alone. I looked through all this data and felt that what I really had was something very important, because I could trace the history of all these various individuals in this survey, and I could see just exactly what motivated them, why they went into the Unification movement, and so on. Then I became interested in slanting the whole book to make a thorough study of the process of conversion. This is what I've really been doing the past several years.

To do this I wanted to use the models given by Lifton, Edgar Shine, Sargant and others who have written extensively on mind control. I wanted to take their models and see how my data fit into those models. I came up with some very interesting conclusions. I found that if you leave off a part of the model they had, you get a very interesting theory of religious conversion which is quite different from what they would consider mind control. So I've come out with the positive result that it is not mind control. What I think I have developed and can prove by empirical data is a theory of conversion, based on needs which are present, certainly, in a period of cultural change such as we have today. The whole phenomenon is examined in terms of the particular changes that are taking place in America today. I'm hoping eventually to get the book finished.

Holly Sherman: My name is Holly Sherman. I was raised in Columbus, Ohio, and I went to college at the University of Colorado from 1967 to 1971. My major was art. I was raised an Episcopalian. I was agnostic during college. Then in 1973 I was traveling up the coast of California, and I was in Morro Bay, and a lady there invited me to come to her church. Though I hadn't been to church in many years, I felt inspired to go. I went and had a conversion experience. It was an Assembly of God church. It gave me faith in God and Christ. Throughout that year I was trying to deepen my faith and find out what it really meant. I went to many different churches and different Christian groups. A year later I met the Unification Church. I went to a lot of the different lectures and dinners and workshops and seminars, and again at one of the seminars I had another experience where I felt very clearly that God was telling me this was where I should be and what I should be doing. That was almost five years ago. Since that time I've really been developing a deeper and deeper relationship with God. That's what has kept me in the Church. I also believe that the Unification Church offers the best hope for the world. I came to the Seminary one year ago. This is my first year, and I have one more to go.

Walter Hearn: My name is Walter Hearn. Ginny and I have been trying to figure out how to identify ourselves here. We have various connections, but we finally decided we should just say we are consultants to Richard Quebedeaux. (laughter)

Ginny and I are a free-lance writing and editing team, although we haven't always been that. It impresses me to hear how "together" everyone here is, even though they are from such different backgrounds. Maybe I'm the first outsider, as it were, because I came from a natural sciences background. I'm a biochemist. You are all excited about theology, but I often refer to myself as a metaphysical minimalist. As a matter of fact, theology in itself is of little interest to me. I'm not sure I'm even very religious in the standard definition of the term. But before I became a scientist, I was a Christian. And so being a Christian, my relationship to Christ has a prior claim on my life. Most people would express that in theological language, I know. In fact I became a Christian when I was very young, probably about 10. I grew up in Houston, Texas, and was introduced to Christ through the Southern Baptists, which many people regard as the poorest way. But I've always been grateful that I spent the rest of my life in a non-Christian world where my understanding of Christ could be sharpened up by being under critical scrutiny of people who thought I was a little off. I spent most of my life in secular universities. There may be some advantage to becoming a Christian before puberty, because it's good to learn to pray under all kinds of internal and external environments. I feel I've learned to pray under fire. Being a Christian in a secular undergraduate school and in the natural sciences was a good experience for me. And being one of the few Christians that I knew at that time in the natural sciences was a good experience. I went on to graduate school, and there I discovered a group called the American Scientific Affiliation which was an organization of evangelical Christians who were scientists and technologists. I became a member while I was still a graduate student. I've been a member for about 30 years now. It's meant a lot to me to know Christians who think and pray about the same questions — especially about the questions that I'm concerned about as a scientist and as a Christian trying to interact with the methodology and data of science.

I did my Ph.D. at the University of Illinois. I spent most of my career teaching at Iowa State University in Ames, although I was also on the faculty of the Medical School at Yale for a year, and at Baylor Medical School in Houston for three years. In 1968, I had a research leave which I took at the University of California. At that time I was investigating a problem that I was one of the world authorities on. Unfortunately, it's a subject that most people find difficult to pronounce, so I won't bring up what it was. One of the authorities was at Yale and I'd already been there. The other was at U.C. Berkeley, so I did my leave out here. That year was the hot year, and especially hot for us because we lived in an apartment on the corner of Telegraph and Haste, right above La Fiesta Restaurant. We had to remember to close the windows before we went to work to keep from being gassed out by the time we got back. We were at People's Park, the second Sunday, I guess, that people were out there working on it. The morning of the great disaster, we were woken up by a noise. We were on the top floor, where the manager had said, "You don't get as much tear gas up here." We thought he was joking when we rented the place. We heard footsteps on the roof that day and it turned out to be police snipers up there. We looked out to see the people putting up the fence and we realized we should get home early that day to close the windows. So we had that adventure in Berkeley. I had let my hair grow long then to blend with the scene, and have saved quite a lot of money since then. My last haircut was in August of 1968 — that's $300 or $400 worth of haircuts.

We went back to Iowa State. The condition of my leave was that I had to go back and teach for two more years there, or else pay back the half salary that they had let me out on. Ginny and I were thinking over our calling as Christians, and we were praying about what we should do with the rest of our lives. We had a strong feeling that we had some writing to do. I had other motivations for leaving the university. One was that I really wanted to work with Ginny. We wanted to share a profession, work together. Although I drew Ginny into my life at the University as much as I could, I always had students over to our home and so forth, she had not been trained as a scientist. So it became clear that if we were going to share a profession, it would be easier to make a writer out of me than a biochemist out of her.

In 1972 we left the University and moved to Berkeley through a remarkable set of circumstances. The Lord found us a wonderful house here; we call it the "troll house" because it looks like it's been built by trolls. And that's where we now do our writing.

Some years ago, in 1967 I guess, we began experimenting with a family-centered rather than church-centered style of Christian life, and we are continuing that experiment. People say, "Where do you go to church?" We say, "Well, we're in a small house church." I have the feeling that what the Lord primarily wants us to do is worship where we live and where we work. If one can find someone to pray with and begin a community of Christ's love with, that's where your energy as a Christian should be focused, your attention should be there. I tend to regard church as a sort of last resort, or third alternative, if you can't do what's really important. And therefore I think there should be a lot of moving across the boundaries of church organizations. No theologian I've ever discussed that with has liked that idea, so I thought I'd throw it in to stir up a little conversation later.

Once I read that at the founding of the Smithsonian Institute, there was a question of what it should be devoted to, and in settling this question, they said people who do science should be interested in three things. One is working out the laws or relationships of science and understanding the principles of science. Doing research, in other words. Another is teaching the principles to people who haven't worked them out themselves. The third is applying these principles to practical uses. I spent 20 years or so working out for myself the principles of Christianity, I spent maybe 20 years or so speaking to people about Christ and what it means to be a Christian, doing some evangelistic speaking, mostly on university campuses. And now I think I'm in a phase in which I'm really concerned to work out, in practical day-to-day life, what difference it makes that a person is a Christian. I'm really concerned with demonstrating that I'm a Christian, rather than advertising the fact.

Virginia Hearn: My name is Virginia Hearn. When I thought about what I would say about how we happened to be at this conference, I said, well, I guess we're here as Richard Quebedeaux's consultants. But I thought further, well, I'm Richard Quebedeaux's spiritual director. I keep exhorting him to pray and trust the Lord that He will provide. And Walter's here as Richard Quebedeaux's economic advisor. We've been in the field of writing and editing for a number of years now and Walt was able to counsel Richard on how to save hundreds of dollars on his income tax.

Herbert Richardson: That's practical Christianity.

Virginia Hearn: I'm another midwesterner. I grew up in southern Wisconsin. I grew up in a family that was very diligent in church attendance, but in a generally liberal tradition. I think in so far as I understood the Gospel through my church background, it was bad news for me, not good news. I thought I had to try very hard to be as good as I could, and if my good deeds outweighed my bad deeds, then hopefully, I would make it in the long run.

I went to college in Ohio, a college vaguely related to the denomination in which I grew up. There, through a dormitory Bible study, the Gospel became clear to me. It became real. Although I wasn't aware of what was happening to me at the time, I would say that that was my conversion experience. I began to read the Bible avidly, and in particular, I was influenced by Inter-Varsity Christian Fellowship (IVCF). There was no IVCF group on our campus, but I read a lot of their literature, and I would say that Inter-Varsity literature preserved me for the Christian faith because it answered the kinds of questions I had. It gave me the understanding I wasn't getting from any other source on that particular campus.

In time I became an editor with Inter-Varsity Christian Fellowship in Philadelphia. I hadn't prepared to go into journalism, but I think I was simply a born editor. In junior high and high school, teachers always pulled me out of the group to rewrite other people's material and to put subjects and verbs together in a coherent and correct way. Working as an editor was a turning point in my life. I didn't know that I was an editor but I really "found myself" in that work. I've been in editorial work ever since.

I have had a sense almost everywhere I've been since then that "the lines have fallen for me in pleasant places."

That's certainly true of our life here in Berkeley and the other places we've lived together. We now do editorial work as free-lancers; we've probably done 70 or 80 books for many publishers, mostly religious, but also a number of secular publishers. We've done such things as foreign language textbooks, systematic theology, books on psychology, missiology, spiritual biography, devotional life, Bible study, eschatology, contemporary issues, you name it. We are the anonymous figures in the background who have polished up the writings of a lot of well-known scholars around the country, and some not-so-scholarly writers.

My own second book was published this year. I've done two books in what you could call the "biography as theology" genre. In the '70s I've also been active in what is known as the biblical feminist movement. I've done some speaking and writing in that area. I'm very concerned about sexism in human relationships and in particular in language. Walter and I are in the process of working out an egalitarian marriage. Many people tell us that our marriage is the only model of marriage that appeals to them, that they personally would find acceptable.

We're also in the very early stages now on two new books. One is on conversion, a certain kind of conversion. I'm going to be spearheading the work on that. We're also going to be doing a book on simple lifestyle. Walter's going to take the lead on that one, somewhat along the lines of Ron Sider's book, *Rich Christians in the Age of Hunger,* but more personal. We're in a phase right now of new directions in our life, because a long-term project on which we have been working has terminated. We're excited about what is ahead, and have seen God bring first one thing and then another to us. We're thankful for that. We have had, as a result of our Christian commitment, an exciting and meaningful life. We're rejoicing in that, and we're very expectant about what lies ahead.

Jonathan Wells: My name is Jonathan Wells. I graduated last year from the Unification Theological Seminary, and am now attending the Yale Graduate School where I'm working for a Ph.D. in theology. It's very interesting for me to be here because in many ways, it's like a home-coming. I dropped out of college in 1963 and became a New York City cab driver. (By the way, I'm a coast man, I'm not a midwesterner.) I became a New York City cab driver, and got drafted. I spent two years in the Army. When I got out in 1966, I came to Berkeley. For a while I sold counter-culture newspapers on street corners on both sides of the Bay. I showed old movies in seedy movie theaters. I finally became a student at the University of California. This was in 1967, the summer of flower children and the swell of the anti-war move-ment. While I had been in the service, I had gotten a good look at the U.S. military and couldn't see any good reason why we should be in Vietnam. So when the Army called me back in 1967 for reserve duty, I refused. What Mark was referring to before was a speech that I gave here at Sproul Plaza in 1968. The day that I was supposed to report for Army reserve training, I gave a speech to a crowd of 1,000 people or so, with TV, radio and newspapers, strongly stating my opposition to the war and to the military. I half expected to be arrested right on the spot, but the Army was too smart for that. At that time, I was living in an apartment over on Northside, Scenic and Virginia, and I was attending classes. One day I walked out of my apartment to go to class. And as I was walking by the Pacific School of Religion, a big black limousine pulled up, three plain clothesmen jumped out, put me in the back seat, took me over to the Presidio Stockade in San Francisco, where I spent the next four months in solitary confinement. I was finally court-marshalled and sent to Leavenworth. This was quite a "cause celebre" because I was a Berkeley student. I went to Leavenworth in 1968, I got out in 1969, and got back to Berkeley just in time to see the beginnings of the People's Park confrontation.

At the time, I was quite active in the anti-war movement and the left in general. But what I experienced during 1969-70 actual-ly soured me quite a bit: the violence and the turn the whole idealistic movement of the '60s took that year. It was an im-portant year for me. It was the year I graduated from Berkeley, but I realized that once we pulled out of Vietnam, the world was still going to have problems. There was more to it than that. I got involved in various Marxist groups, including the Communist Party, because actually that was the only viable alternative, it seemed to me. I found that these were the people who were really serious and far-sighted about the social changes that were going on, especially here in Berkeley in those days. I found them impressive for their seriousness and dedication, but ultimately heartless. The best thing I can say about the ideology that was motivating them is that it was heartless. That, among other things motivated me to move out of the Bay Area and head for the hills, literally. I went to Mendocino County and became part of that counter-culture scene and grew my hair long. Up to that point I looked like I do now. I lived in communes and started reading all the books that people read in those days, and still do. One book I read, in particular, was called *Be Here Now,* which some of you have seen. It is a book that's a blend of Hindu, Buddhist, Christian, Confucian, Judaic andTheosophic ideas. But the thing that impressed me was where the author quoted from the first commandment: "I am the Lord thy God. Thou shalt have no other gods before Me." And I'll never forget the day I was reading that page, that particular page, up in the mountains of Mendocino County. I was completely by myself and really praying and trying to understand where my life was headed and where this country was headed. That one sentence struck me so powerfully, that it was at that point that I began to believe in God. I put aside all those Neo-Buddhist, Confucian and Hindu books and read the Bible. For the next two years, as I lived again in various locations in Mendocino County, I devoured the Bible and fell in love with it and prayed. I just loved Jesus so much, partly because I could really empathize with what He went through, having gone through on a much smaller scale a similar idealistic, self-sacrificial journey of my own.

At the same time I was consciously looking for spiritual companions. In Mendocino County at that time there was a powerful Jesus commune. I also had contact with the Guru Maharaji's group and I had contact with the Unification Church. I was weighing all of these alternatives in addition to many others. I had come from a science background. What I felt myself looking for was a spirituality that was faithful to my reading of the Bible, faithful to my scientific background and also adequate to this need that I felt for social change in America, the need that the communists were unable to meet. The Jesus People that I met there didn't have it because somehow their ideology was too much in conflict with my scientific background, and the feeling I got from them was just a bit too dogmatic and exclusive. The feeling I got from the Guru Maharaji people was one of peace and love. But it didn't have any backbone to it, and

therefore couldn't provide any kind of foundation for social
change. But the Unification people had somehow just the right
combination. The more contact I had with them, the more
impressed I was with them as people. I should point out that my
first contact was hearing a lecture by Dr. Durst in Oakland. Then
later I heard Rev. Moon speak at Berkeley. And finally, after
about a year and a half of praying and reading the Bible and
checking into all these different groups, I decided to join the
Unification Church. That was in 1974. So since that time I've
been doing the things that Moonies do. Since going to the Seminary, I've been to a number of these conferences. In fact I was at
the first one that Darrol attended. And I find them to be constantly a surprise, because something new happens in each one
of them. They're never the same. So I'm looking forward to this
one as well.

Neil Duddy: My name is Neil Duddy, and I come from a
fairly a-religious New England family in Massachusetts. I grew up
in that kind of environment; but just as I was heading off to the
university, I began to consider the person of Jesus. A number of
my friends were grass-roots Christians. I thought about it for a
while. I took the very simple approach of a teen-ager thinking
about who Jesus was: either He was somewhat deluded, a de-
ceiver, or telling the truth. I thought His life backed up the
notion that He was telling the truth, so at that point I had a fairly
good conversion experience.

When I was going to the university, I tried to build a bridge
between my academic studies and my faith. That forced me to
do a lot of double homework, and I didn't find I was able to
come up with resources that were adequate. So I went to a
seminary in Philadelphia, Westminster, and was encouraged in
building that bridge. It was a very constructive time, and I think
what helped me most during that time to prevent my faith from
becoming an exercise in mental gymnastics and scholasticism,
was that I became involved with Young Life and Inter-Varsity.
They had social concerns, and there I found some pretty good
avenues for living my faith, and from that I developed a view of
how the mind really works: an understanding of human rationality mixed with some of the other pleasures of life—like Woody
Allen says in *Manhattan,* the noncognitive things of life. I got
married, and the marriage was very good, too.

At that point we were interested in going to Nigeria. About a year later I was going to be involved with an indigenous seminary there doing New Testament studies. Then they had a couple of political *coups,* and we lost contact with the folks that we were interested in being with. We worked in a church in North Carolina for about a year. The work went well, but it lacked some of the qualities that I think were most helpful to Linda and me, and so we came to Berkeley. I'm currently interested in new religious movements from the sociological perspective—that's been pretty engaging for the past several months. Linda and I have just finished a book on Witness Lee and the Local Church*, a theological overview on an odd sociological group. My particular point of interest this weekend is hermeneutics. Our time in Nigeria would have been spent studying contextual hermeneutics; what constitutes Christo-paganism or indigenous Christianity, and cultural influences on different themes in Scripture. I'm interested to see how the Unification Church relates to that. I hold the biblical affirmation that we were created in the image of God, that all men are valuable and should be upheld and honored. And in that spirit, I'm interested in open and honest communication.

Linda Duddy: My name is Linda Duddy, I'm a transplanted Easterner having been raised mainly in North Carolina and Virginia. My spiritual pilgrimage has been a quiet one. I was raised in a home with Christian parents. I regularly attended Sunday school and vacation Bible school. As an adolescent I had a very emotional attachment to the saviorship of Jesus Christ, but it wasn't until I went away to the University of Wisconsin in Madison, in the Bible study of Inter-Varsity Christian Fellowship, that I found an intellectual affirmation of my faith and my commitment to the lordship of Christ in my life. Seeing how I'm one of the youngest people in the group, I don't have an extensive background career-wise or educationally. Neil and I moved here approximately a year and a half ago.

For the past year I've been working with a Christian countercultural newspaper called *Radix,* formerly *Right on,* and I've just left *Radix* to do some editorial work I want to do and the change will also give me a little more free time. I look forward to attending some New College courses and dabbling in hobbies now. I'm here

*Neil T. Duddy, *The God-Men: An Inquiry into Witness Lee & the Local Church,* Downers Grove, Il.: Inter-Varsity Press, 1979.

primarily because I not only like to read about such movements as the Unification Church, but definitely need to attach warm human beings to the theology to keep things in perspective.

Yoshihiko Masuda: My name is Yoshihiko Masuda. I was born in Japan. My family has an eclectic background: Buddhism, Confucianism, Shintoism all mixed together. In my family there's a Buddhist family shrine, and a Shintoist one as well. In daily life we practice Confucian ethics. In my high school days I was interested in Christianity and I read many Christian books. Then I entered Tokyo University, majoring in political science. I wanted to become instrumental in building a better society, or ideal society, so I wanted to study how to build the ideal nation and the ideal world. Right after entering the university, I was wondering which club I should join. That was 1965. CARP, the Collegiate Association for the Research of Principles, the student club of the Unification Church came to campus and spoke. I was very impressed. When I attended a Divine Principle lecture, I was invited to a one-week workshop. I attended it and was very moved. I was impressed by the character and personality of the members. I was invited one month later to a two-week workshop, and I decided to join after those two weeks. That was my freshman year. I moved into the CARP center and one year later, I worked for a year as a pioneer missionary in Japan. Then I returned to the university. I graduated and worked as a director in a local Church center. In 1973 the Unification Church invited 100 Tokyo University — mostly graduate — students to America for the first International Leadership Seminar. I came as one of the staff for the 40-day Seminar. The Japanese students studied in the Bay Area. After the seminar, I was supposed to go back to Japan, but Rev. Moon told me to stay here in America. I've been working in America since then. I attended the Unification Theological Seminary and graduated with its first class. Since last September, I've been studying at the GTU, doing historical studies as a first year M.A. student.

When I entered Tokyo University, I was attracted to Marxism. There were communist groups there, but I was very disappointed by them. They were violent and so divided. Even though they all believed in Marxism or communism, they were always fighting and kicking one another. In seeing their character and personality I was very disappointed. At that point I attended a Unification lecture, and I agreed with the purpose of the Unification

Church. I, too, desired not only the perfection of the individual, but also the perfection of the world. You should reach a goal of individual perfection, as well as the perfection of the world. I liked this purpose very much. I wasn't sure about the details of the theology at that point, but I agreed to work with them. Also, Christianity when it came to Japan didn't emphasize the importance of the family, and so there had been conflict with the predominant Confucian ethics which are very strong. Unification theology emphasizes the importance of the family, and there's very little conflict. I like that point. Shintoism is almost dead in Japan, but Confucian ethics remain strong. Confucianism is not treated as a religion: in high school and junior high, Japanese youth study Confucianism as classic literature.

I've worked in the Japanese Church for eight years and in America for six years. I was married two years ago and now I have a little baby girl, 10 months old. I am very happy to be a member of the Unification Church even though there are many controversies surrounding it and we are sometimes persecuted. I have great hopes in the Unification movement. I'm very excited to be here tonight.

Mike Mickler: My name is Mike Mickler. I'm also a student at the GTU. Here in the Bay Area, I've had the opportunity to speak in a number of classrooms about my experiences in the Unification Church. So I've shared my story a lot, and I'd like to do it as briefly as I can here. Harvey Cox wrote a book that came out a couple of years ago called *Turning East.* Maybe some of you know that book. He said that young people who joined new religious movements, particularly Eastern groups (the Unification Church wasn't mentioned) were looking for three things: first, "guru" or teacher, second, "dharma" or teaching, and third, "sang ha" or community. As I reflect on my experience, those are the things that I was looking for.

I'm from the Midwest, Cincinnati, Ohio, and my family was non-religious. The kids were to make up their own minds. I went to Wesleyan University and majored in English. I did an M.A. in English at the University of Cincinnati and taught freshman English for two years. At the end of that time, I was at a spot where I had to think about what I was going to do. I did not want to go on for doctoral studies at that time, but what was I going to do? Actually, there was nothing to do. I wanted to make a contribution but there seemed to be no outlets. I was rather miserable at that point. I had no larger meaning or structure to my life. Then I happened to pick up one of the Don Juan books by Carlos Castenada and began reading metaphysical literature. I had been depressed to think that reality was solely physical, and that this was all there was. Reading metaphysical literature was my quest for "dharma," credible teaching or interpretation of reality. Also, I decided that I needed a teacher. I felt very acutely that I needed personal guidance. At that time, I was into Ken Kesey. He had led the "Merry Pranksters" in the Bay Area and his story is chronicled in the *Electric Kool-Aid Acid Test* by Tom Wolfe. I decided, "I'm going to find Kesey." Since I wanted to be a writer, I thought I could be his disciple. I wanted a community as well. My family had no church or religion, and we had no larger community with which to relate. My parents had friends, but we just weren't integrated. I had thought of joining an Israeli kibbutz.

In that spirit, I traveled to the West Coast and ultimately found my way to the Bay Area. I went to Palo Alto where I worked unloading trucks. I roomed with a guy who was using marijuana and LSD, and I felt I should explore this too. One night we took LSD. I had never done that before. It wasn't having any effect, so I went to sleep on the couch. I woke up at 11 o'clock and the LSD was having a tremendous effect. I felt very disoriented; I got up and walked to the bathroom and looked in the mirror and it wasn't me. That was the bottom line. Here I was already miserable, and now I didn't even have control of my faculties. That was the end. So, what did I do at that point? I don't know why I did this, but all of a sudden I just started calling out for Jesus, just like this, "Jesus, Jesus, Jesus, you've got to come, you've got to come." Right away, immediately, at my right shoulder was an incredible presence. I knew it was Jesus that had come to me. I didn't see anything. There wasn't any visual imagery at all, but I knew it was Jesus. An incredible sense of peace radiated out toward me, and love. I was really moved by that, and also then Jesus bent over and whispered right into my ear some words. What He said was, "I am your big brother." That's all. "I am your big brother." Those words really struck me, because I'm the eldest son in my family. I have three brothers and one sister, but I had never had an older brother. I was the first to go through everything. It didn't matter: adolescence, dating girls, shaving first, everything. It was a joke in my family. I found it difficult to go through these transition phases. I always wished I had an older brother to go through first, or to help me through. So when I felt Jesus say that to me, I felt "Wow! *Jesus* is my older brother!"

That was very, very meaningful, but it was not a conversion experience. I was not about to go out and join a church. It was a wonderful experience, but I had nothing to integrate it with. Jesus was great, but that was it. Then the whole cycle started over again. A week later I thought of going down to Los Angeles, but then I got this urge to go to Berkeley instead. That's where I met the Unification Church. I really feel saved by the Unification Church. There I basically found a lot of things I was talking about, a teacher, and a community. More importantly, I was also opened to a continued experience of Jesus Christ. Since joining, I've attended our Seminary, and now I've come to the GTU.

Mose Durst: My name is Mose Durst. I'm the director of the Church here in Northern California. From a very early age I was aware of being a Jew, since my family was Jewish and since I grew up in Williamsburg, (next to Jerusalem, Williamsburg is probably the most orthodox Jewish community in the world). I was aware of the outer trappings of Judaism, and also the inner ethical sensibility. From a very early age I was also aware of the split between the desire to create an ethical community and the world I lived in. My dad had grown up experiencing the war in his town in Europe. The Jews had suffered so much. I was always aware that the Jews were isolated as a people. I always believed that there had to be an answer to human suffering, and there had to be a relationship between the Jewish experience and the non-Jewish experience. The first thing my grandmother taught me was, *man darf sein ah mensch* (Yiddish phrase). "You have to be a human being, you have to develop an ethical sensibility, an ethical perfection." The second thing she said was, "Look out for the *goyim*." I knew clearly that there were two worlds. Whenever the name Jesus was mentioned, it was as if he were the cause of all Jewish suffering.

I went to school at the City University in New York. I hung around with New York intellectuals. There was always a taboo subject, and that was the subject of Jesus and Christianity. We just never got onto that subject except in joking; it was never taken seriously at all. I tried in my own life to somehow resolve the problem of human suffering. On the one hand the Jewish people spoke about the messianic age, the idea of building God's ethical society in the world, of enjoying the world. On the other hand there was the paradox of tremendous suffering. Writers and literature offered me the best insight into the nature of life and the nature of suffering. So I studied literature. I went on to graduate school, eventually to Cambridge in England, studying literature. I began graduate school with a fellowship in medieval studies. I thought the medieval world offered the best, coherent picture of life. But I came back from Cambridge interested in modern American culture. I did my dissertation in modern American literature. I eventually got involved with the discipline of psychology. After I got my doctorate, I studied a little bit with Abraham Maslow, and was concerned with institutional change. I did some therapy work in Lewisburg penitentiary. I got involved with the anti-war movement and Marxism. I found that there was a certain violent heartless quality in the midst of Marxism that did not solve my personal desire for ethical perfection.

I now teach literature at Laney College in Oakland. I developed an inter-disciplinary studies program there. My hope was that by creating learning environments that were healthy and creative, people could feel healthier and more creative. But, as I was discussing at dinner, somehow the teaching profession left some things unresolved. It didn't have enough impact. There was something missing in my relationship to the world, community, family. Eventually I got involved studying spiritual things. I think it was always a quest for unresolved community. That has always been a hunger in my life. In my studies of 19th century American literature, I was always fascinated with utopian communities. While they didn't always get it together and often went and hid away from the world, I thought they were asking the right question, "What is a healthy community?" I liked studying with Maslow because I felt he was asking the right question, "What is a healthy person?" In college, I was always fascinated with Martin Buber as a theologian because he was asking the question, "What is a healthy basis of relationship to the world?" And it was to him as a Jewish theologian that I could relate most clearly. Eventually I met my wife-to-be, an early missionary of the Unification Church here in America, who came to San Francisco in 1965. Through her I was moved as to how a person could be so devout, so good as a human being. I met our movement here when it was a very small community. The people were living the ideals I had always talked about in my teaching. I studied the Principle, and for me it was a rigorous intellectual challenge. I was involved, in Mike's sense, with a search for a teacher and a teaching. My wife was an example of a human being I had never seen before: someone whose heart and life were completely devoted to making her ideals real. On the one hand, here was a simple person; on the other hand, I couldn't match her wit or her understanding of life. Her sacrifice in Japan as an early missionary and her hard work in this country put me to shame. The good things that I thought I was doing in my life were nothing compared to what she was doing, even though she didn't have the same intellectual background as I had. It was completely moving to me. The spirit of our community in those days was what brought me through a conversion experience. It was a conversion, actually, of Christian love. I never understood the meaning of Christ's love for the world until I encountered the Unification Church, and it just completely exploded my previous concepts. My whole life opened up in new dimensions. Of course, as I said, that had been an area of complete taboo for my life: to understand the meaning of Christian community. The realization that God's ideal could be made real in the world, and become the foundation of family, community, relationships, professions and the intellectual quest just completely opened up new horizons for me. It allowed me to build on the best of what I had from the past and to discard the worst. It gave me a framework to be much more discriminating in every way, in a much more loving way, in a much more committed way, in my intellectual quest and in my community building, my Kingdom building, my personal relationships, my responsibility.

Then eventually, I became involved with the direction of our church here. I'm involved with many projects as a teacher, a husband and a father. It's been a very challenging experience and quite a journey. I never would have anticipated it, especially the last few years with all the tremendous persecution. This has involved my coming to terms in a very disciplined way with what it is I believe, what I'm trying to create. For me the Unification movement offers a way to deal with the suffering of the world. And yet we bring about suffering to other people as well as joy. How to deal with that paradox has been a tremendous challenge in my life. But all of these things have made life more interesting than literature. That's part of my answer to the question why I'm here.

Patricia Zulkosky: My name is Pat Zulkosky. I'm a second year student at the Unification Theological Seminary, and next year I'll be going to the Claremont School of Theology for graduate studies. I was born in Seattle, Washington. I grew up in South Dakota. I was raised a Catholic, and it was a very important part of my life. I went to Mass and communion every day during one year, and I thought about religious community quite seriously. I also had a lot of questions. Just simple basic questions, like, "How can I really rest my faith on the Bible as divinely inspired?" Or, "How come if God is good, He can allow the world to suffer so much?" In the course of my asking questions, I had one man tell me to stop asking questions in class because I was destroying the faith of the people in my class. That destroyed my faith, because there just weren't any answers that I could find, even though I kept looking for answers. I wanted to commit my life to God, but I just couldn't find the answers that would allow me to do that. From there it became a very piece-meal search to know God. I eventually became involved in the more Eastern kind of tradition and the whole idea of perfection became the most important thing to me. I embarked on a plan of how to become perfect by just taking a quality which I considered part of perfection and working on that until it became part of my life. I believed that at least by the end of my life I would have made some progress that I wouldn't have made otherwise. Part of that was for me a real community outreach. I went to the University of Washington and graduated in occupational therapy. At the same time that I was doing that, my apartment was a drop-in center for about 12 or 15 people. Sometimes as many as nine people were staying there, from an ex-con to a foster daughter. We had the most amazing little community in my apartment. It was all part of trying to reach out to the world and trying to alleviate the suffering of man.

Perfection was my life, it wasn't just my profession. I was in the final stages of getting my degree when I met the Unification Church. The person who met me was witnessing for the first time in his whole life. He was quite scared and didn't make any sense. He mentioned the word "perfection," but basically I was filled with compassion because of his effort. I was into giving people success. (laughter) This boy obviously needed support. I was the first person that he had ever talked to, and it took all of his courage to even talk to me. So I told him I would come and hear the ideas that he was talking about, to give him value in his life. The community that I met was unusual to me. At that time there were about twenty people living in a two-bedroom, one-bathroom house, and it was so meticulous that you would have never guessed that there were so many people living there. The house was completely clean and the harmony was beyond belief. It defied every principle of psychology that I knew. I was used to community living, but this was very unusual. It struck me that these people were closer to perfection than I, and I was consciously on a course of trying to become perfect. So I wanted to know why these people who were so close to perfection would gravitate together. And they kept saying, "Well it's not that we gravitated together, we are people like everyone else, but because of our beliefs we have purpose and value in our lives." I was skeptical but I just wanted to know what allowed them to be that way. As I listened to the lectures, I found answers to many questions I hadn't been able to find answers to in my search, answers to questions about the authority of Scripture and the whole question about good and evil. It struck me that through this kind of cooperation centering on God and an ideal, there was much more potential for making a big impact on the world beyond what I could do as an individual therapist. For that reason I became involved in the Unification Church. Since that time I spent a little time in Palo Alto, I was in Chicago for about 18 months, and I did some pioneering in the Church as an individual missionary in Maine. I was a state leader and lecturer in the Church for a long time for the 7-day and 21-day workshop. I was an assistant to Mr. Sudo, one of the Church leaders, for a couple of years before I went to the Seminary. So I had a broad range of experiences, especially in relation to education. In fact, my Master's thesis right now is on teaching people how to lecture the *Divine Principle,* and on developing a method to educate our own members to become more verbal in their faith.

I hope to be involved in the field of religious education. It's very important for me to take spiritual principles and develop them in a very practical way that can help people change their lives and change the world. I have a great love for theology, but not just for the abstract elements of theology, but how we can take theology and apply it to religion and let it become alive in the lives of people. In the Seminary, I've been involved a great deal with conferences, working especially with Dr. Quebedeaux. We're an evangelical conference team! It's been a very exciting thing for me to see how people live their religion in different traditions. I see a mission of reconciliation developing in a very strong way through education and dialogue. I'm very excited to attend this conference because I will be coming to California in the fall and I hope somehow to be very active in the Christian community here.

Richard Quebedeaux: My name is Richard Quebedeaux. I was born in Los Angeles as was my father, which is rather rare. I have a father who was a cultural Presbyterian and a mother who was a lapsed Roman Catholic. My father's ancestors settled in Louisiana in the early 1800's of Huguenot stock. I am a mixture of every conceivable thing. On my mother's side, I'm German and Dutch. My mother and father wanted me to go to Catholic school, but that was not possible. My parents eventually went on a spiritual quest. My father started reading Plato and got into Aldous Huxley. They went from church to church, and finally he went back to his Presbyterian roots. I was baptized for the first time in the Presbyterian church in California. As a result of Sunday school, and having gone to a Christian day school when I was very young, I have just come to realize that I have always understood myself as a Christian.

We moved to Columbus, Ohio, for a year, and finally resettled in Long Beach, California. My parents wanted to find a Presbyterian church to join. They had become quite avid churchgoers. We were in a neighborhood where there just wasn't a Presbyterian church. So they just waited for the Presbyterian church to be established. However there was this woman on the corner who was a very fundamentalist Baptist. My parents were big party people, and they always had the best New Year's Eve parties. This woman, of course, never came, because she was sort of a religious kook. She worked on my parents, saying, "Why don't you come and visit our little church?" She worked and worked and worked for about a year, and finally since there was no Presbyterian church nearby my parents and their friends agreed one Easter Sunday — I think I was in the fourth grade — to go to church. My father cussed all the way because he couldn't find it. But they went there and boom!—they both were converted. I went down the aisle, too, at their instigation. All I can remember is that my counselor had very bad breath. It was nothing new to me, I was always a Christian. But my parents changed dramatically. Of course, they stopped the New Year's Eve parties in the neighborhood, and I didn't like that very much. And they also stopped drinking and smoking and everything else. My father started tithing. Consequently, I was raised in the First Baptist Church of Lakewood, California. I did everything. I was president of every group all the way up. I was a camp counselor. I taught Sunday school and sang in the choir. I led a double life. I was the master of the double life. I had a car when I was 16 and I used to go down to the Rendezvous Ballroom in Balboa, with my church friends and down into the surf scene, all the while I was with the church. I went to a Christian high school and also led a double life.

In my tradition, *the* place to go was Wheaton College in Illinois because Billy Graham had gone there. I was groomed to go to Wheaton. I gave testimony in front of my church and went off to Wheaton in 1962. I lasted one week. All the freshmen I met were talking about just one thing—how to lead a double life, how to go into Chicago incognito on the weekends, and where on campus you could do certain things. Luckily I had applied to UCLA as a back-up. I called them up. Fortunately they hadn't received a letter I had written saying that I didn't want to come. So I enrolled three weeks later. I called up my folks and said, "I'm coming home and going to UCLA." They sent me the money, I came home, and they marked the day as my decline into liberalism! I had left Wheaton and gone to UCLA.

At UCLA I went through the usual political transformation. My father's family was politically on the right and he was a very rugged individualist. My grandfather on my mother's side was an avid socialist who helped many people leave Germany as Nazism arose. My mother's family was as left as my father's was right, which is why I'm right in the middle. I decided I was for Lyndon Johnson in 1964, and that was a crisis for me in my church and in my family because I was leaving fundamentalism, number one, and political conservatism, number two, and that was very bad. At that time I also became heavily involved in the academic thing, and I started associating with secular Jews—the people in the History Department at UCLA who were the most interested in academics. I was influenced by a man in the History Department who was a Catholic church historian and who had participated in an ecumenical dialogue at Harvard in the '60s. In the course of my time at UCLA I drifted away from my home church because I was a heretic by their standards. I was politically liberal, theologically I was still orthodox. I was in medieval history and I wanted to go on. So I applied to do a Ph.D. at UCLA under Gerhart Ladner. Ladner told me that I really needed to get some theology if I wanted to do church history. I had always thought of seminary because that was part of my tradition. I thought there were only two or three seminaries: Fuller Seminary, Dallas Seminary, and Bethel Seminary in St. Paul, which is the seminary of the church I grew up in. So I thought I'd go to Fuller. I went out to Pasadena, was interviewed and was totally turned off, and said, "My God, I've got to find somewhere else." So I checked out Harvard. I wrote a letter to the registrar and said, "Could a person with a background as conservative as mine possibly be admitted to Harvard Divinity School?" I got a letter back from them saying, "It just so happens that the Dean of Students is interviewing at UCLA." So I was interviewed and this guy turned me on. So I applied and was admitted. I had to break the news to my parents, because my father had to pay some bills, and he and I did not have a very good relationship because of politics and theology. If I had wanted to go to Union Seminary, the "Red" Seminary, it would have been "No, no, no, no!" But when I said Harvard, it was OK. My parents felt "Well, you know, it's too liberal, but we can tell all our friends our son went to Harvard." So I went there.

I guess I was looking for what I didn't get in my background. I was looking for an open place where people were open to other people. I had come from a very sectarian tradition. I didn't even know there were real Christians who weren't conservative Baptists, really, until I got to college. But when I went to UCLA I discovered other Christians. I went to Harvard looking for what I didn't find in fundamentalism because of bigotry, narrow-mindedness, etc. I went to Harvard, and I found what I call a fundamentalism of the left. Instead of openness, I found a very narrow perspective held by most of the faculty, only the enemies were different. I noticed that on all the reading lists very few conservative books were listed. All of a sudden I began to identify with everything in my evangelical tradition that I thought was right. I was one of the only "uncloseted evangelicals" in those days at Harvard Divinity School.

I got to the point where I decided that either I was going to give up the Christian faith, because I had seen both sides, right and left, and both were sickening, or I was going to find a new synthesis. I had some kind of a conversion experience at that point where I decided I was going to be a Christian, and that orthodox Christianity was the only thing that made sense to me. It was a personal decision, and I've never really veered from that. I set out on a quest to bring together the best elements of Christianity as I understood it to make a whole. For instance, I always thought that my fundamentalist, evangelical background really helped me to know how to get in touch with God (the vertical dimension). And I felt that my liberal friends—many of them—really had it together in terms of how to relate to the world and to other people (sort of the horizontal dimension). I came, in the years after divinity school, to think that the solution was to integrate what I call the personal and the social dimension of the gospel.

When I was in seminary, my parents went one step beyond the Baptists, they became Pentecostals. That was a real shock to me. When I came home they took me to Pentecostal services. They got me going to Kathryn Kuhlman services. It was fascinating. Here was an example of Pentecostals and Charismatics getting together with Catholics. It was very open in character. I had always wrestled with my Catholic and Presbyterian roots. And as time went on, I became involved as a sympathetic observer of Pentecostalism and Charismatic renewal.

By a quirk of fate, I left Harvard and went back to UCLA to begin a Ph.D. in medieval history. But seminary had made me more interested in the present than in the past, and I didn't want to spend the rest of my life reading Latin manuscripts in libraries. So I finished my M.S. there and got a scholarship from the World Council of Churches to spend a year at Oxford. I took a leave of absence from the Ph.D. program at UCLA and went to Oxford and didn't have anything to do. I was tired of lectures. So the Principal of my college, John Marsh of Mansfield College, said I should find somebody to supervise some reading for me. I ran into a guy named Bryan Wilson who just happened to know a lot about Pentecostalism. I had talked with him one evening for about three hours. He was impressed by my knowledge of the new Charismatic movement in the main-line denominations. He said, "Why don't you do a Ph.D. here?" I said, "Well, I'm only here for one year, I've only got money for a year, and I wasn't admitted to do a degree." Well, Wilson took everything in hand and the result was that I began my Ph.D. at Oxford. I decided that I would do a doctoral thesis on the Charismatic movement. I spent two years there, and came back to the States in 1971, just after the job crisis hit. I still hadn't done much on my dissertation, but I was on the job market, and I spent a year or a year and a half not being able to get any kind of job at all, even though I thought I had really accomplished quite a bit. I became rather depressed. I was sitting home with my parents. We were still alienated by politics and theology. It wasn't a happy situation. The only surge of inspiration I got was a television program called "The Hour of Power" with a man named Robert Schuller. I watched that and he kept talking about things like, "If you ever find yourself in front of a mountain and you can't get over it, just dig a gold mine in it." You know, crazy stuff. I said, "Well, maybe I am too negative. Maybe I should be more positive. Maybe God is really behind me." I had a friend who was up in Berkeley, studying at the GTU, and the principal of my college had told me that if I ever got to Berkeley, I should look up John Coleman Bennett, who had been president of Union Seminary and who was teaching at the Pacific School of Religion (PSR). I was up in Berkeley in the fall of 1971 and called up Bennett. He invited me to come over, and I had a three-hour conversation with him about an article I had read in *The Christian Century* that said a big evangelical conference named Urbana '70 (run by Inter-Varsity) was really getting socially concerned. Billy Graham hadn't been invited because of his hand-holding with Nixon. Tom Skinner, an eminent black evangelist, was castigating evangelical churches for racism, and there were several speakers who were against the war in Vietnam. Bennett had not read the article and was fascinated. He said he had never known any socially concerned evangelicals, and asked if I would be willing to write an article for *Christianity and Crisis* on this new social consciousness of evangelicals. I hated writing. Nobody had ever told me I was a good writer, but I knew this would be published. So I went down to the UCLA library and spent five or six hours writing the article. It was published in the back of an issue in December 1971. Three months later I got a letter from Harper & Row asking me to expand that article into a book. Well! I didn't have a job, so I rented a dorm room at UCLA, and wrote the history of my spiritual pilgrimage in a book that I thought would really solve the major problem of Christianity by integrating the social dimension of the gospel with the personal dimension. We could have a righteous world order with a whole bunch of people who were saved and knew Jesus. It was a passionate book. I was embarrassed by the book, but I turned it in anyway to the publisher.

In the course of writing the book I had met some campus ministry people. I was invited by them to speak at a campus ministry conference, and my task was to tell all of these people what the evangelicals were like. At that conference I met a campus minister from the University of California at Santa Barbara. He invited me to spend a year at Santa Barbara in campus ministry while he was on sabbatical. My task was to bring together the conservative evangelical campus ministries and the liberal main-line and Catholic ministries. That was in 1974. I went there and began to flesh out what I had written, and it was successful. I got liberals and conservatives together for the first time, just to talk about what they were doing in terms of ministry in Santa Barbara. And they liked it. My book came out the end of April that year. It got a lot of publicity, including a lead article in *Christianity Today* on the day it was published. All of a sudden, all of these people I had written about began seeking me out. I didn't even know these people personally, but they all assumed I was traveling in evangelical circles. At that point I became a celebrity among a small group of people I called the young evangelicals. We were all really seeking the same thing. We all loved Jesus and we wanted to do something in the world, and we didn't feel that those two things were mutually exclusive. We got together and a movement grew. My success in Santa Barbara in bringing together conservative and liberal groups led me to get a job with the Southern California Conference of the United Church of Christ to do the same thing. They wanted to get to know Fuller Seminary which was right next door. So I brought them together

and put together ecumenical-evangelical conferences for ministers. Then I was hired by the United Church Board for Homeland
Ministries to do the same thing for a couple of years nationally.
In the course of all this ecumenical work, I became a professional
writer as well, and that's basically how I live, although I don't
really like to write that much. A lot of people might envy me as a
free-lance writer but I always wanted to be a professor.

For years after I wrote my first book, and my second book,
and my third book, I became almost bitter. Even though my job
was to bring Christians together, I was somewhat detached from
everything I was doing. It felt good to see people come together,
but I was on the fence, so I was doing these things out of my own
principles and to enhance my reputation. I had a lot of bitterness.
I was bitter at the liberal theological institutions that had turned
me down for a job because I was a white male. I was bitter at the
Evangelicals for not thinking I was really a Christian. I felt that I
was better than everybody. I moved to Berkeley in 1975, and I
made Berkeley my base of operations with the United Church of
Christ, and in my writing.

But, anyway, how did I get involved with the Moonies? You
all know that Berkeley's been a center of the Unification movement.
Ever since I got to Berkeley there were tables on campus and
very nice people and a bus called "The Coffee Break". . .every
conceivable Moonie operation. I couldn't have cared less. I
wasn't negative, I wasn't positive, I said, "Well, Rev. Moon's just
another false messiah." One rainy Christmas day I was walking
to see some friends across campus, and I saw a group of people
who were singing Christmas carols. They had umbrellas, and
they were out in the rain and I said, "God! There's only one
group that would do that!" The same five or six people that were
there every single day! It somehow moved me. It's sort of silly,
but here were some people who were trying to brighten up the
day for a few street people who had nowhere to go on Christmas
Day. I said, "Well, you know, that's interesting." But I sort of
forgot about it. I left the Moonies alone. I never talked to them.
They were there, and that's fine. They're kooks, and that's OK. I
just tried to avoid them as I went across campus almost every day.
I knew if I looked at the table or stared one in the eye, they'd
come over, and they'd probably walk across campus with me,
and I didn't want that. I avoided them.

I am basically a free-lance writer, but because I'm also an

academic, I got involved with people at the GTU. Then I got
involved with a friend of mine who was a doctoral student at
GTU, with a new Center for the Study of New Religious Movements. In fact, my friend was a student of Stillson Judah's. Through
him I became a member of a seminar which Jacob Needleman
started on new religious movements. I remember going to the
seminar with my friend once, and a stranger walked in, and my
friend said, "Oh, he's with the Unification Church." "Oh, he's a
Moonie!" I said. He kept saying, "Well, his name is Mike." I kept
saying, "Well, he's just a Moonie!" But in time I got to know
Mike Mickler as a friend. I was writing a book on Bill Bright and
Campus Crusade and I really needed to go back East and interview
Bill in Washington. But nobody was paying my expenses. Mike
knew I had a book coming out, *The Worldly Evangelicals,** so he
set it up for me to lecture at Barrytown at the Unification
Seminary, and then I could go meet Bill at Unification expense,
so I thought this was a nice coup. Although I wasn't very interested,
I agreed to lecture at the Seminary on the Evangelicals and my
book, and also to go to a theological conference led by Darrol
Bryant, who had been in seminary with me. So I gave my lecture
on the Evangelicals, and I couldn't for the life of me figure out
why people were so interested. Then I met some professors, and
went to this theologians' conference. The atmosphere was really
interesting. The people were very nice and hospitable, and there
seemed to be quite a bit of freedom. I didn't see anyone "brain-
washed." Hardly any of the faculty were Unification members,
they were all from other persuasions.

Somehow in the course of these early days—and it may have
been Mike's idea originally—I went away from that conference
with an invitation to put together a dialogue with Evangelicals
and Unificationists. I was very high leaving there. It's a very
interesting environment. You never leave there the same way as
you came. When I left, I experienced culture shock on the train
from Barrytown to New York City. I was so high. I said, "My
God, what did I get into? I have to invite Evangelicals to have a
dialogue at the Unification Seminary. Who in the world am I
going to get!!?" So I started trying to get my "left evangelical"

---

*Richard Quebedeaux, *The Worldly Evangelicals,* New York, N.Y.: Harper &
Row, 1978.

friends, and they weren't interested at all, because Moon is an anti-communist. I called one of my more conservative friends from Campus Crusade, and he said he would love to come. Then I talked with his boss in Washington: "Hey, guess what. I'm putting together this little conference, and guess who's coming, your personal assistant." Bill Bright answered then, "Oh, fine, great." Well, that gave me some encouragement, so I called some other people and finally got a group of ten people together. We met in June of last year. As a dialogue, it went like this: there's two parties, an evangelical party and a Unificationist party and one or two people in the middle, and we had a four-day meeting. Everybody liked it so much that we all decided we wanted a part II. Those two dialogues will be coming out in a book* published by the Seminary. After that, it was decided that I should put together more evangelical dialogues for the Seminary. So I decided that since the first two dialogues were basically made up of Reformed evangelical people, I would have a Wesleyan-Arminian evangelical dialogue. Then we had one with Evangelicals from England and a dialogue with Pentecostals and Charismatics. Just like Darrol, I've been in Barrytown seven or eight times in the past twelve months and I have never been bored. It's one of the few places I have the opportunity to discuss theology seriously. That doesn't happen in most seminaries or in most of my circles. A lot of people think I have converted and am trying to subvert the whole evangelical community. It's very hard to do anything for or with the Unification Church without having people think you are being used, or brain-washed, or converted. I've never had anything to lose because I'm a free-lancer, and I can do what other people can't do, and I rather enjoy it. I think that if you want an interesting religion, this is it.

But what is it that really attracts me? Well, I have to confess that despite my theological disagreement with Unification there are certain things that really attract me. It's kind of a product of pilgrimage. First of all, community. I have never known a church that had the kind of community that I think is fundamental to—at least as I understand it—New Testament Christianity, as much as the Unification Church. Now, I've seen the best—I think

---

*Reference is to *Evangelical-Unification Dialogue*, Richard Quebedeaux and Rodney Sawatsky, eds., New York, N.Y.: Distributed by the Rose of Sharon Press, Inc., 1979.

that probably the best and the brightest tend to be at Barrytown. That's an academic bias. But I've seen a community there of very highly idealistic people who make me believe that community can happen and that it can be very good. Secondly I have seen, much to my chagrin, people who are much more socially concerned really, in terms of putting lives on the line, than the liberal people with whom I've been dialoguing about social action for years; people who are literally willing to give everything they have for the realization of a just social order. In being with the Unificationists and seeing what the opposition against them is like, for the first time in my life, I've come to appreciate my Baptist roots, because the Baptists originated in an ethos of religious persecution. Now I know that religious freedom is very, very important. It's something that, even though I was raised a Baptist, I had never really appreciated. I could tell you a lot more about the kind of things that have happened to me and to my friends whom I have brought to the Seminary. For years I've tried to bring liberals and Evangelicals together in dialogue, and it was always the Evangelicals telling the liberals what they believe, and the liberals deciding whether they could tolerate it. Every dialogue I've put together at Barrytown has been very good, because it's a real intellectual dialogue between two groups of people who think that theology isn't just important, it's of *ultimate* seriousness. People accuse me of being used, but I would say that in many ways the people who come to Barrytown at Unification expense are using Barrytown as much as Barrytown is using other people. I have been criticized for, with whatever notoriety I have, legitimizing Unification. All I can say about legitimacy is that every person is created in the image of God and is legitimate. Unificationists are so legitimate that Christ died for them. And that's the only way I can approach that. I think the whole issue of legitimacy and illegitimacy is a social thing. We all know about the unjustified stigma that 'illegitimate children' have to bear. So that's why I'm here as a participant in a dialogue that Darrol is putting together. I'm very happy to be here. I'm glad to hear all of your testimonies. Through the Unification movement I too have learned to give a testimony again. (laughter)

Herbert Richardson: I can sense, Richard, that Pat Zulkosky is really working to give you a sense of success. I want her to go to work on me! (laughter)

Darrol Bryant: Matthew and Tony, we're going to let you each say a brief word. We're already some time beyond my original promise that we would quit at 10 o'clock.

Matthew Morrison: I'm from Michigan. I grew up in the country and studied ecology. At the University of Michigan in 1968 similar things were happening as in Berkeley. My center was out here in Berkeley at the time. I felt as I studied that it was the beginning of the ecology movement, and I really had a deep desire to do something for the world. At that time, my approach was the approach of natural science, how to manage natural systems. I found very early in my study of ecological systems that they were doing just fine by themselves. They didn't need any management, but human beings needed management. So the question of ecology was more a social question or a question of human ecology. The problem of man and nature was just part of the deeper disease of man's relationship to man. I participated avidly in the radical politics of that time. May Day in Washington, D.C., in 1971 was the last straw for me. Then, I finally decided that it was not working. I decided to be truthful to myself and to pretty much leave society.

From there, I went to Alaska where I spent two years trying to find my way. Somehow I felt I had been born 300 years too late. I had missed the frontier. The only place I could feel any sense of God was in nature. There I found my ideal: being dropped out of a helicopter and left in the wilderness. I had been doing wilderness surveying in towns and Eskimo villages above the Arctic Circle. I was in places where I lost radio contact with the world. Once it happened that I was without food or anything for exactly 40 days. Eventually, during that experience, I came to a point where I began to think for the first time seriously about my life. I saw as I reflected back on my experience that if my life ended at that moment, I wouldn't really have accomplished anything. I had sensed my whole life that I could do something great. But I didn't know what it was or how to do it. At that point I could see that everything I had done in my life, I had done basically for myself, and that to have a significant or meaningful life I had to do something for the sake of the world. At that point I really promised God that if I survived, I would do something for the sake of mankind.

During that time, my older sister, who was living in Berkeley and doing a Ph.D. program in psychology, gave it all up and was living, like Jonathan, in a tree-house in Mendocino. There she met the Unification Church in Booneville. After this experience of travelling 400 miles by foot in the wilderness and finding an old trapper's cabin, I felt truly I had been given my life back by God. After this experience, I came down to California and at that time the community at Booneville was just seven people. Three of them were my sisters. It was an amazing experience. I thought they were very naive, believing in such ideals. Either they were naive, or they knew a lot more than me. I wasn't sure which. I sensed a quality or nobility in each person that so fascinated me that I wanted to have it, I really wanted to have it in my life. Through my experience growing up in the Unification family, and getting to know Dr. Durst's wife, who has become my guru in a real way, I was able to really discover God. The quality of a truly religious life was so amazing to me. We would get up every morning and go to the top of San Francisco, to Twin Peaks, and we would pray for the sake of the city. We would pray that someday, every light that was still glimmering, every household, every person, could somehow appreciate their lives fully, that somehow every human being could know God. It was so moving to me.

My mother was the director of religious education in our church, and my father was a mush-heart. Every time we went to church, he just cried, so he didn't go any more. The music was so moving to him. My parents were very skeptical about Rev. Moon and the Church for many years. They had all four children in the movement. Finally, after seven years, my father came out here and had a religious conversion experience in a dream, a vision, and realized this was the purpose of his whole life. That was just last year. It was an amazing experience for me, after seeing their negativity for a long time.

I've been here in the Bay Area for almost eight years now, and I've felt perhaps the most powerful thing in my whole experience has been an incredible love for America. In my prayer and in my lecturing I have come to really feel the tears of God at seeing the potential of America flipping out, of seeing my own generation completely spaced out, not realizing that we are a chosen people, in a sense blessed of all the blessed on the face of the earth, having every conceivable thing and not knowing what to do with it. That's been the primary motivation in my life the past few years. In lecturing and other things I am trying to help people understand the value and the potential of this country. I feel that being able to live a deep religious commitment 24 hours a day is something that is truly wonderful. I feel that the whole basis of religion is to move the heart of God. If I, in my own personal life can move God's heart, then in a sense the whole world can turn. That's been my goal in my own personal life: to see how, in a life of complete dedication I can move God's heart. In moving God's heart, I feel that the whole world will change. I'm really grateful to be able to hear everyone's testimony.

Anthony Guerra: I had from a very early age a tremendous interest in the question of God. When I was growing up, I went to a Catholic elementary school, but was turned off to my own religion at that time. I responded by becoming a sort of Bertrand Russell skeptic. I went to a parochial high school that demanded compulsory Mass attendance. Let me tell you a story about it which captures an aspect of my personality. I ran for president of the student body in high school. This was a Catholic boys' school. My major platform was to do away with monthly com-pulsory Mass attendance. We had a nominations committee meeting at which all of the students and faculty and administration of the school got together. Each of the nominees was supposed to give a speech. I had a friend of mine take a picture of a lamb from the school yearbook and make a big reprint of it. I began my speech by holding this over my head, and saying, "Here, this is what the administration of this school thinks of you. They take the parable of the sheep and the shepherd a bit too literally, and guess who the sheep are in their eyes?" The result of that was a kind of dead silence on everyone's part. In the ensuing conflict between the administration and myself, they refused to print my speeches in the school newspaper along with everyone else's. The reason I want to tell you this story is because it says some-thing about where I was standing spiritually at that point. About two weeks after I had lost the election by a few votes, I was called out of my homeroom down to the principal's office, where he said, "We're seriously thinking of expelling you from school." I was completely surprised. I was a senior, I had been accepted to a number of colleges, I was second in my class. I asked why, and he said on the grounds of blasphemy. He explained to me something which I was unaware of at that point, that the picture which was reprinted from the yearbook was actually the image of Agnus Dei. At that point, one who knew me might have thought that my reaction would be to say, "Well, look. So what?" But I was completely silent at that point, and although I didn't say anything, I realized at that moment that my particular complaints towards the Catholic Church were in spite of my deep, personal love for Jesus Christ. To me, that was a kind of internal, private Protestant reformation.

In any case, that event, and a number of other events, led me to later renounce my skepticism and become open to religious thought again. Eventually through this process, I met the Unification Church. After studying the *Divine Principle* for a number of months, while attending the university, I joined the Church. Even though I joined it, I lived outside the community for a few more months. Since then, let me say that the Unification teaching, particularly on the nature of atonement, explains certain unresolved questions about the meaning of Jesus and His crucifixion, and the salvation that He offered, which allowed me to accept it, and accept the messianic position of Jesus. I've done many things in the Church. I've been head of the church in Massachusetts, and in Nashville, Tennessee. I attended the Seminary in Barrytown and graduated last year. I'm presently at Harvard Divinity School.

Darrol Bryant: Well as Richard said, this is a very amazing set of stories. Many people talked about conversion experiences. I'm one of those people who have never had one. I grew up in a Christian home, and I've always experienced myself in that way. And I was thinking tonight, "Well, what kept me in the Christian faith?" I think that what it was, was my final year in college. I spent a year trying to figure out what was the matter with Anselm's proof for the existence of God. I decided at the end of the year that it was really — given a couple of qualifications — true. And that sort of stands as a pillar in my life, after which God's existence has never been a question for me. Anyway, this has gone on much later than I had anticipated. It almost inevitably happens this way, but I'd thought I'd introduce Anselm in the conversation at this point, by way of suggesting that tomorrow we will talk about the theology of the Unification Church . . .

Hermeneutics: Opening the Question

Darrol Bryant: From our introductions last night, it strikes me that we might fruitfully focus our conversation on the question of hermeneutics. That's a many-sided question and I'm sure that different people conceive it in different ways. Since Mr. Duddy was the first to raise the issue last night, we'll let him begin.

Neil Duddy: First, I would like to say something about the record of Western theology: it is often akin to a speeding pinball machine in which there is a lot of action-reaction. Many theologies developed as bouncing defense mechanisms. There's an emotional attachment that many people have to theology that leads them to use theology as a defense mechanism. Of course everyone would like to believe that they are using theology constructively: helping people in their everyday situations to be more progressive and social, and working toward alleviating the problems that the world presents us with. Still, theology is often used as a defense mechanism. In my particular background, that's what it's used for primarily. Therefore, Western theology has pretty much confined itself to a heady propositional emphasis. Things that don't come across as being purely propositional sometimes create a lot of problems. However, it's interesting to notice that in different cultures that don't have the same kinds of Western problems there have been different uses of theology. Some of these different uses of theology come about just by the cultural context in which people live. For example, there are different geographical areas in Africa where the future tense isn't part of their grammatical structure. How in that context do you go about communicating the notion of the coming Kingdom of God, when we will see the satisfaction of God's reign on earth? This raises the problem of what I would call cultural or contextual hermeneutics. This would involve questions of how people see things, and how they perceive the Gospel, and how they communicate the truth of Scripture. There are cultural orientations that bring out different responses to different elements of the Scripture. For example, in the West because of our strong traditions of individualism we would have more of a tendency to think of the church in terms of individual commitment. But some of the Africans that I've met from Nigeria and Uganda have a tremendous sense of community. There are instances where whole tribes would get evangelized and no one would step forward when there were "altar calls." But if the chief did, this was the same as if everyone did, and there was a tremendous spiritual revival. Here then is a sense of social solidarity, a sense of community, that would shape their understanding of the church.

Now this is a starting point of my interest in the Unification Church. It has its roots in Korea. Have they, given this background, responded to different elements of the biblical Gospel? Have they just expanded and built on those truths in Scripture which in Western thinking might be considered secondary or tertiary truths? Could the differences of cultural backgrounds be a source of confusion when the Unification Church moves into a Western context?

Anthony Guerra: I think that's a very perceptive comment. And, I think you are right. For instance, the whole notion of yin-yang which is very tied up in Confucian concepts is used in the *Divine Principle* to explain an aspect of the divine nature which is manifest in the creation. We see these aspects of masculinity and femininity in Adam and Eve and believe them to be characteristics of the divine nature that are present in all of creation. For instance in the Unification view, we believe that in order to bring about the ideal world, we need a family centered on God. The family is the key. The meaning of the Adam and Eve story is the coming together of man and woman to create a child. But since that didn't happen *properly* you need a savior to come, and that savior actually has to be again both a male being and a female being who cooperate together to bring about salvation. Therefore, in the Unification view, the Holy Spirit, like in Eastern Orthodox theology, is a female agency. Also the Unification view holds that Jesus and the Holy Spirit, as the father and mother, generate a spiritual love which, when a person takes the child position to Jesus-father and Holy Spirit-mother, leads to rebirth. You see the same thing in our eschatology. The Second Coming is also going to be Christ as the third Adam, and his bride as the third Eve, who will generate a family of a new order that can begin a new age. So that this Eastern notion of masculinity and femininity becomes integral to the whole theology of the *Divine Principle*. So I think that's one way in which one can see the influence of Oriental culture on the theology of the Church. There are probably other aspects as well.

Theologian X: Just in looking at the *Divine Principle* and following the yin-yang principle within world history, and also the assertion that Jesus' success was spiritual only and not yet physical, it seems to me that logic would require that the Lord of the Second Advent will have to be a woman. Yet it didn't come out that way. I was just kind of curious why the Lord of the Second Advent is assumed to be a man?

Anthony Guerra: Well, first of all, according to the Unification view, Jesus is the Messiah, but the Holy Spirit also has a salvific function. This is what I just explained. So that spiritually you get a spiritual father who is Jesus, and you also get a spiritual mother who is the Holy Spirit.

Theologian X: The way I interpreted it was that the Holy Spirit was the spiritual side of the physical Jesus.

Anthony Guerra: The Holy Spirit is an independent agent, independent, that is, of Jesus, who cooperates with Him through a relationship whereby they generate spiritual love which offers rebirth to the Christian who stands in the position of child to Jesus-spiritual father and Holy Spirit-spiritual mother.

Herbert Richardson: I would be inclined to say that the Lord of the Second Advent is a woman in Unification theology. Let me explain. If one moves to a higher level of abstraction as we do in theology and does not use the word Christ but uses the phrase "the christological symbol complex," what are the elements in the Unification christological symbol complex? It's clear that in Unification theology, as in Catholic theology, there's both a man and a woman. The suggestion is that in the Second Coming, there must be...

Theologian X: You're speaking of Mary now, I assume.

Herbert Richardson: Yes, in Catholic theology, there's Mary as well as Jesus. One sees this development in, for example, the iconography of the Catholic crucifix where you see the increasing presence of Mary.

Anthony Guerra: I think that what you have in Unification is a specification of what divine love really is. Of course, the phrase "Lord of the Second Advent" is used, but that is a suggestive, open-ended title. What it suggests, I believe, is that the messianic function, or the salvific foundation, is now going to be performed, not only by Eve and Adam, but by men and women in their relationships to each other. This is what I mean by saying that in Unification theology there is a specification of what divine love is really like. The best analogy of divine love is the love between a man and a woman which is pro-creating love. I think that traditional Western Christianity, because it lacked the woman figure in the christological symbol complex, had to use heroic action as a model of what divine love is. Go out there and sacrifice yourself.

I think one could ask, on a theoretical level, what the appropriate human analogy is for speaking about divine love? In Unification theology it is the relation between a woman and a man. This becomes for us a theological way to talk about divine love. When you see this then you understand why the family is seen as the critical point within the *Divine Principle.* The critical point within the world where divine love can enter is through the love of man and woman, and their love for their children. I think that's the doctrine.

Now to return to Neil's question, you can ask where did that doctrine come from? Here's what I think happened. I think it's a precise reading of the Scripture in an Oriental context, where the notion of identity is so familial that people think of themselves as *members of a family.* Hence, if they were to sin, rather than saying, "Oh, I feel so guilty, I sinned!" — that's an individual approach — they would say, "Oh, what shame I've brought upon my mother and father, my brothers!" The sense of being a member of a group is so much stronger that the problem of guilt is less important than the problem of shame. Hence, when you read the Scripture, you're always thinking in terms of the family. So, when you go to the Adam and Eve story and read that Adam and Eve sinned, in the West we always say, "What did they do?" And you immediately turn to questions of responsibility and guilt in Adam and Eve. But in Unification theology which is so much more Oriental, you ask when you read that Adam and

Eve sinned, "What's that going to mean to their family?" So then you look immediately to Cain and Abel to see the effect. The reading of the effect of original sin in the family context takes you into looking at Cain and Abel, which it seems to me is a perfectly legitimate hermeneutical move, given the Eastern familial cultural pattern. It generates, however, a new theological datum from the point of view of Western theology because we're so individualistic. That's what you said about the African world. I've always found that to be a very useful insight into how people reading the Bible in another culture with a different anthropology discover in the Bible new teaching that the Western church didn't see.

Durwood Foster: I think the discussion is illustrating the complexities of the hermeneutical problem. Hermeneutics is such an oceanic problem that it is difficult to know where specifically to begin. It seems to me that one of the issues that immediately faces one is how one goes about attempting to differentiate between the *realities* one is seeking to construe, understand, appropriate, and integrate, and on the other hand the *conceptuality* of the symbol complexes within the group in which one is attempting to do that. This is not at all easy. It's like splitting the atom. The realities — if I may use that word without being challenged with respect to it — we are talking about, are already merged into and mingled with symbols that we use to talk about them, and yet we know they're not one and the same. Hence, they must in some way be differentiable.

In addition, I wanted to raise the closely connected question of how one who is not already in the hermeneutical circle of Unification theology goes about understanding the inner logic of that theology? It seems to me that Mr. X's question was oriented in that way. He extrapolated from an analysis of the deficiency that is found to exist in the case of Jesus, to conclude that logic would seem to demand that the Lord of the Second Advent should be a female figure. To pose that kind of question is potentially fruitful, hermeneutically, for those who are not within the circle, because to think through that kind of issue with Unification theologians would give us some concrete feel for the way you think and for the frame of reference, or the field of force, within which you are moving.

Now, specifically on that question, I had an observation also. I didn't follow the process of extrapolation that Mr. X went through, because it seems to me — and correct me on this because I haven't reviewed recently the specific data — but as I recall, what is found to be specifically deficient in the case of Jesus is the early termination to which His historic life and career comes. That is, He is crucified before He can, in fact, carry through as presumably He otherwise would have, and generate a family, a new humanity in the physical sense. Hence, what is needed now is not simply a woman to stand alongside a man, but what is needed is a new beginning — someone who will carry through what Jesus was prevented from doing because of His early death. So the logic would seem to entail, in this case, someone like Jesus in many other respects, who doesn't get crucified quite so early. That would seem to me to be within the framework of the existing argument.

Anthony Guerra: I would agree. But I want to enlarge this discussion. I must speak confessionally as well as theologically, because part of my struggle in accepting Christian teaching before I joined the Unification Church was this: how could a loving God demand the death of His Son as the only means to salvation? That was a gut-level reaction I had against the Catholic interpretation which led one to believe that of God. I wouldn't subscribe to that.

What Unification theology did for me was to explain that God, in His love for His created children, limits Himself to the point where He responds to as well as acts in history. Human beings can respond to God's intervention in human history either positively or negatively. So when God through the prophets prepares the historical foundation of a nation to which to send the Messiah, all along the way they have the decision to accept the prophets and then to accept Jesus, or not to accept them. God's desire is that the people will receive the Messiah, that the Israelite nation will whole-heartedly accept and unite with the Son of God who represents the new humanity, who is the embodiment of the new humanity. It's by people uniting with Him that they can gain awareness, be educated, and receive a new spirit in which they too can be renewed.

So the major point in Unification theology is the unity between the Messiah and the people. How that unity would come about is a major point. The unity could have come about, Unification theology says, by people simply following and obeying Him. After He'd taught them, they'd say, "Yes! Here's a man of

God, here's a person to whom I should take the child position, the student position — with whom I should work." Or if that doesn't happen then there has to be another means, and the alternative becomes the crucifixion, where by that utter sacrifice Jesus demonstrates a kind of love and obedience which is so persuasive, which is so powerful an example, that after the resurrection people realize who He is. They were not able to realize who He was without the event of the crucifixion, but that was not God's primary will; that was the historical situation.

So, in Unification theology there's the notion that there is a God who is working within history but is limited by the responses of human beings. Somehow that view seemed to do two things. It seemed to say that the crucifixion wasn't the only way, but at the same time it upheld the value of the crucifixion under those historical circumstances. That explanation solved a very critical problem for me.

Herbert Richardson: In this case, your way of presenting the doctrine of atonement is a little like the game that many theologians play: they caricature the position that they are now not going to accept to make it easier to reject it. Though I think it's a reasonable caricaturization you've made, I just want to ask you this question. One of the nice things about having Evangelicals here is that it's a reminder to stay close to what a good evangelical interpretation of atonement might be. Now, speaking from this point of view, you used two words to describe the Christian doctrine of atonement which you were going to reject. One was, God demanded this of His Son and sacrificed Him and the other was that the act of Jesus Christ was an act of obedience to God.

Now, I would just like to say two things. First of all, at least within the longer Catholic tradition, God the Father did not demand the death of His Son, but the Son freely and voluntarily sacrificed and offered up His life to God as a sign of respect, hope and love for the Father. That's the first point. And the second is, the death of Christ is not any part of the obedience of Christ to the Father, because the Father cannot demand of a sinless man that he should accept death. The real freedom of Jesus to give His life to the Father is a free act over and above obedience since God doesn't have the right to demand the death of a righteous person. Now in the Catholic tradition, it's fully understood that Jesus offers His death to God on our behalf, as our brother, out of love for us and because He honors the Father.

And if I may say this, what kind of a God would it be who would reject a gift like that? See how the rhetoric gets turned around? Suppose that my son goes, and out of concern for my purposes, sacrifices his life, and I say, "I reject any gift like that." Ridiculous. I would say, "My son, how you've loved me, how I rejoice in this gift, and how the honor you have given me is truly yours not mine." Now, I think that that's the true Christian doctrine of atonement, and also that it is a fair account of how Unification theology might interpret the death of Jesus, namely, as something offered to God out of love.

Now, why has the problem you allude to, Anthony, arisen? The problem arises, I think, because what happened in the Christian tradition is this. Christians began interpreting the meaning of the atonement in terms of the verse John 3:16, "For God so loved the world, that He gave..." So the death becomes something, then, that the Father gives rather than that the Son gives. I think a real deformation occurred there. Although the verse is all right, many people didn't reflect on it properly and consequently a certain authoritarianism entered in. I think that Protestantism has a lot of concern for command ethics and obedience, rather than for an ethic of sacrifice and gift, and that this to some extent depreciated and distorted the death of Christ. They wanted to make Jesus' death an act of obedience, rather than an act of love that was beyond obedience, which is a supererogation which we Protestants aren't supposed to believe in, but which seems to me exactly what's at the heart of the classical doctrine of atonement. Now I think that the Unification criticism of Christian theology is in fact Unification criticism of certain forms of deformed Christianity, and in that way it's a useful criticism. What I think I've said, namely, that the death of Christ is the Son's offering to the Father, has to be understood as an act of filial love and respect, and not as a work done by obedience. It's a free and gratuitous gift. Can Unification theology accept that account?

Anthony Guerra: Let me say that I really thank you for that interpretation because I think you're accurate. In the New Testament we find a number of interpretations of the sacrifice. Certainly in the Pauline tradition, we do have God as the agent of salvation and Jesus as the instrument, and I was describing one tradition that came down to me within a Catholic educational system. Maybe they were deviant Catholics? (laughter) But I think that the description of the tradition I was talking about is close to the evangelical position. You're probably right in saying the view you offer is the traditional Catholic point of view.

Unification theology talks about the intimate relationship the historical Jesus had with Heavenly Father. They were in communication with each other. If you read the *Divine Principle,* it talks about the Garden of Gethsemane scene where Jesus was communicating with His Heavenly Father about the crucifixion itself. In the Garden of Gethsemane He was asking if this was the only way. I don't think that Jesus got the idea at some point that He wanted to make this offering to His Father...How can we work this out?

Darrol Bryant: Careful now, are you shifting there to a caricature of another position? I think that a couple of things are getting confused here. If we go back to Neil Duddy's question, the question involves the impact of specifically the Korean cultural context on the emergence of the *Divine Principle* and on the formation of certain Unification doctrines. I think that's a very important and interesting question and some things have been suggested about that that are very illuminating. That is the context out of which this religious movement has arisen, and there are built into that setting certain kinds of metaphysical assumptions related to yin-yang, family, traditions, and so forth that affect the reading of Scripture and the presentation of the theology of the *Divine Principle.* I think we still haven't explored that whole question sufficiently. There's another set of problems, though, and I think those are also important. When we encounter this movement in the context of North America, especially in the context of people trained in the Christian traditions of the West, there is a whole set of other problems that arise. The thing that you said that struck me earlier was at the end of your statement. You said something like, "And that means we believe in the notion of a limited God." Why did that come in? What's that related to? Is it related to Eastern metaphysical notions?

Anthony Guerra: I guess it was a question for me. I said I was going to speak confessionally, and to me it was a problem. I'm sorry, I in fact wasn't answering your question, but I thought the question had gone through three or four permutations by that time.

Darrol Bryant: Well, it has gone through about three or four permutations. I'm just trying to sort some of them out, so we can focus on them one at a time. Perhaps we should simply go back and ask other Unification members here to address themselves to that specific question Neil asked, about whether or not the Korean cultural context has played a significant role in the formation of the *Divine Principle* and Unification theology.

Dagfinn Aslid: Actually, what I had in mind was less specifically the Korean element than — the word I've had on my tongue now for a little while is the word, "history." It is a very important category for our hermeneutics, and speaks to the relevance of the Bible. Now I grew up in a context where I had the Bible all along. I grew up with the Bible, since I grew up a Christian. But it didn't have any relevance; it didn't address the secular situation or the philosophical systems that I encountered. It's the historical hermeneutic of the *Divine Principle* that opened up Scripture for me in a new way. It allowed me to bring the biblical categories and biblical stories into a meaningful dialogue with people I met on the street. Then I felt comfortable in bringing out the Christian faith. This new understanding of Scripture forced a wider horizon, so to speak, in my faith.

If I were to address the question of the Korean element in Unification theology, I would see that as the historical event of two horizons meeting, East and West. I think we see in the *Divine Principle* a complex merging of those two horizons.

Yoshihiko Masuda: It might be possible to say that Unification theology is orientalized Christianity. I can see as I said earlier certain similarities between Confucianism and Unification theology. In Confucianism, the important concept is parents and children, the father-son relationship and filial piety. In Confucianism the central figure is always expected to function as a father figure. In Japan, our members are supposed to be symbolically parents and children. In a Japanese company also, the president is expected to function as a father, and the employees as children. Many Japanese and Koreans have this Confucian concept. Because of this concept many Japanese and Koreans tend automatically to interpret Adam and Eve as parents. Jesus is also in the position of a parent. Naturally, when I read the Bible I felt it was strange that Jesus didn't establish a family. For many Japanese it is very strange that Jesus didn't establish a family. One of the reasons that the Japanese rejected Christianity is that the New Testament teachings didn't stress the importance of filial piety. So for many Japanese, Christian teaching is not ethical; it is morally unacceptable to Oriental cultures. Rev. Moon was brought up and educated in Korea and Japan, Far Eastern cultures. I can see some influence of Confucian ethics. I think Rev. Moon studied Confucian teachings in elementary school and junior high school and high school — especially in those years, students were required to memorize important Confucian sayings or teachings. Therefore, there may be some Confucian influence in Unification theology.

Stillson Judah: This has been very interesting to me, but I'm wondering whether there really isn't a different impulse motivating the Church here in America that is quite different from that of the Church in Korea. In other words, in Korea you have the very interesting mixture of Christianity with Confucianism, the yin-yang philosophy, and other things which make Christianity more acceptable to the Oriental eyes. In America it seems to me, the main thrust is in a type of work ethic for bringing in the Kingdom. Actually you have then a very important part that is played by those who are in the American Church who seek to bring in this Kingdom itself, to work toward it so that they are, through indemnity and making proper conditions by their sacrifice, bringing about the conditions that will make possible the arrival of the Kingdom. I try to see this in the context of my own surveys of the people in the Unification Church. One of the things that came out very strongly in the national surveys we made was that the Unification Church members had a high percentage of people who were involved in demonstrations. Considering that the period that the surveys were made was in 1976, that far removed away from the real period of the demonstrations, this would mean that they are extremely socially active people who believed in the '60's that they could by their work and effort bring about great changes here in America. Of course, we're all aware of the idea of the Revolution that was going to change everything. Well, after the 60's the demonstrations largely stopped, but it seems to me that in the Unification Church you have a transference of this same zeal to bring about these changes, but now sacralized, as it were, through the work ethic of the Unification Church. It seems to me that this is one of the reasons that the Unification Church has a special attractiveness to the people who join it.

Theologian X: Let me just get some clarification here. Are you suggesting by implication, then, that the Unification Church in the United States with this work ethic context would be different than the Church in its context back in Korea or Japan?

Stillson Judah: Yes. If I understand Masuda correctly it is the combination of Christianity with the Oriental yin-yang philosophy and Confucianism that makes Christianity acceptable to them. I see that in the United States it is not the Confucian ethic, it is not the yin-yang philosophy that is so important, (except of course, the male and female content is very important right now in our own society because of the conditions) but actually here those people who have found importance in the Unification Church are those who were socially active in trying to bring about changes, through demonstrations which failed in the 60's. But now it's a similar but sacralized notion of change in the Unification Church that attracts people.

Patricia Zulkosky: I don't think you'd find a great deal of difference in terms of the work ethic in America and Japan or Korea. Bringing in the Kingdom is a major theme around the world. It's not something that's specifically American or Western. And I do think that some of the Oriental influence on Christianity through which Rev. Moon has made the Bible come alive is a very important thing for Americans. Before I met the Unification Church, I couldn't find an explanation that suited my nature, or dealt with the different aspects that I really felt I needed to deal with. Some of the things that Masuda is talking about are things that I was looking for. They are lost elements of Protestantism in America. There seems to have been a time of strong family ties and loyalty in the States, but these have fallen away. The Unification movement led in me to a rebirth of concern for the family that I think isn't uniquely Confucian. I think there's a stream of that even in American thought. The Unification movement led, in me, to a rebirth to that standard of hope and idealism. I don't think you'd find a big difference in terms of those particular dynamics.

Jonathan Wells: I think the discussion is relevant and very interesting. The fact is that the Oriental elements are there. But to relate back to Neil's original question on hermeneutics, it seems to me that on the hermeneutical level, we are dealing with two very different matters. I wouldn't want to say the *Divine Principle* is simply a Christian gloss on Oriental philosophy. This discussion has brought out that this is not the case. So the question is, what is the hermeneutical approach? How is the *Divine Principle* derived from the Bible? If I can dissect Mr. Duddy's question a bit, I think you were proposing an answer to a question that you implicitly hinted at, but never actually stated, which is that there is a very pronounced difference between Western theological traditions and the *Divine Principle,* and that is the issue. Now, by Rev. Moon's own account and the account of early Church members, the way that Rev. Moon derived the *Divine Principle* from the Bible was not by mixing together various elements. At an early age he began "crying." In fact, the early Church is known as the "crying Church," because even after it got started the Church services were just drenched in tears. Rev. Moon and the members cried not just out of repentance, but out of concern for mankind. And not even just that, but out of a concern for God. So the hermeneutical approach that Rev. Moon used was to read the Bible in order to learn how to comfort God. The story that I heard was that he went through many Bibles. He wore them out; they just fell apart because he devoured them trying to understand what God was really trying to tell us in the Bible. Now, there's the whole issue of the clarity of Scripture. Isn't the Bible obvious? Can't you just read it and it's clear? I hope we don't have to get into that. If the Bible were clear, Western Christianity would have been thoroughly united from the time of the first ecumenical council. That's the point we have to get at: Rev. Moon wanted to find out what God's point of view was when the Bible was written. Whether he's right or wrong is another question, but that's his hermeneutical method.

Darrol Bryant: Is that his hermeneutical method, or is that the question with which he approaches the Bible?

Theologian X: Could you restate your last two sentences, I missed part of one of them.

Jonathan Wells: His purpose was to find out what it is that God is trying to tell us in the Bible, granting that it was the word of God. There are clearly things that don't seem to fit together, and things that seem to be left out, additions and clarifications that need to be made. So he wanted to clarify the basic questions of the Bible, not just coming from the Oriental cultural viewpoint, not just for the purpose of establishing a certain kind of theocracy, but as nearly as possible to find out what God really wanted to say. So he takes the Bible very seriously. The Bible, to Rev. Moon, is much more important than Confucian philosophy, infinitely more serious. But the way it is viewed is as an imperfect record written down by people, many of whom didn't understand what God was trying to say. Obviously we have to interpret it and the *Divine Principle* is the outcome of that.

Durwood Foster: I'd like to make a very specific comment on this point. To me it's part of the hermeneutical complication that exists for us as a problem. I like what you said in terms of its illuminating the situation of Rev. Moon. But one observation that needs to be made is that the Christian community of faith had for two millennia been in that situation and recognized it as such. It recognized that there is a problem of understanding what God wishes to say to us in the Scriptures. And there is an immensely rich and substantive theological tradition that has been generated through those two millennia attempting to answer that question. At least *prima facie* one has the impression that Rev. Moon did what we sometimes accuse biblicist denominations of doing. As Paul Tillich would put it, he simply jumped back over two millennia, as it were, directly into the Bible and started there. Now that is perfectly understandable psychologically, but he was not conversant with these two millennia of rich theological tradition, at least not very deeply conversant. Maybe I am wrong about this. Maybe he was more conversant than one has the impression he was. It would be an interesting question to me just how much of the history of classical Christian theology Rev. Moon knew. But I can say that he plunged into the biblical text itself, in going through various versions.

Jonathan Wells: Yes.

Durwood Foster: OK for me, there's deep pathos in that image. But I haven't heard anyone say that, in any comparable way whatever, he went into what for most of us who work in the established Christian tradition is also a definitive hermeneutical frame of reference, namely these two millennia of theological interpretation. I guess I'm saying something very obvious. One of the gulfs that we face is that those of us in established Christianity who want to relate to Rev. Moon's witness are doing so out of these two thousand years as it were, and he is doing it in a more direct way and with a more — not to use the word in a pejorative sense — primitive biblical stance of his own. This is just an observation, but the question in it is whether anyone here knows whether and how and to what the extent the Rev. Moon was theologically educated, in addition to going through these many versions of the Bible.

Herbert Richardson: I want to say something to your question specifically. We began with Neil's question about the Korean context and how it might have influenced the formulation of the doctrine of the Church. We immediately began discussing — which is perfectly all right — Korean family structure, yin-yang, and so forth, totally forgetting that Moon was a Presbyterian. He was taught Presbyterian doctrine, he was taught the Westminster confession of faith, he was taught his Christianity by Presbyterian missionaries who were trained in the United States, who brought the entire American Reformed Presbyterian theological tradition to him. So when he read the Bible, he didn't read it as some person who found a Bible in a bottle and read it on a rock totally out of contact with the Christian tradition. He read the Bible that was given to him by Presbyterian missionaries. There were obviously competing Christian missionaries in town, and anybody who knows Korea knows that there would have been arguments among them going on. Moon's formulation of doctrine is discussable among us precisely because it is a formulation of doctrine growing out of and in direct relation to discussions about doctrine in the American Protestant tradition. Probably it was a context that focused especially on the argument between the perfectionistic Baptist-Methodist group and the Reformed group, perhaps somewhat more along dispensationalist lines. Here the central questions were the meaning of the atonement and the work of Christ. These questions, these doctrinal positions that the Unification Church throws out, I think have to be understood as what a Korean who's joined an American Presbyterian church and listened to other arguments about which formulation of Christianity is right and studied the Bible now says to this discussion. My belief is that Moon learned a bad Western doctrine of atonement from his missionary preacher and read the Bible and talked with others and said that's not the doctrine of atonement the Bible teaches. The Unification people today say, "We've got this great new doctrine of atonement, which is different from the Christian view. However, I believe that the doctrine of the atonement that is implicit behind Moon's critique is really what I would call the bad doctrine of atonement that they were getting from some local preacher. That's what I think.

We all know that Unification theology is exciting to discuss precisely because it has the same contents as Western theology. Why does it have those? It has those because it's formulated in direct relation to the theological discussion going on in Korea at the time it was being developed. It's perfectly obvious that, historically speaking, Unification theology poses its questions within the framework of on-going Protestant theology, not Catholic theology. That's the whole *Fragestellung*. When we go into the question of the hermeneutics in Korea, while it's certainly true that Korean culture is one factor, no less important is the Christian missionary situation there out of which Moon comes and to which he responds. That's the second thing hermeneutically.

The third thing hermeneutically is this. This is the Jonathan Wells approach. In the Korean tradition — and interestingly enough this is another thing it has in common with the American evangelical tradition — there is the belief that you can commend what you have to say by making it clear that it rises out of deep sincerity and goodness of heart. It's usually emphasized by offering a dramatic contrast by saying, "Well, he used to be very insincere and nasty, but now he's very sincere..." Now, I may say, as a Presbyterian minister, I think all of this talking about how sincere you are and how much you prayed and whether you had dreams or not is a bunch of nonsense. Nuts are sincere, and Hitler was sincere, and they all cried. And so what. There's a kind of pietistic subjectivism here. I recognize its legitimacy. But I want to say that I'm much more interested in the question about what the Scripture says, about being true to Scripture. I don't care how much you cried before you found the answer. You could have cried all night and still have a wrong answer. That's part of hermeneutics, too. The pietistic hermeneutics says that we have to hear that Rev. Moon cried. I think that's sweet but it doesn't convince me. What does convince me is a theological argument.

Now here we have the fourth thing. Formally, I think Rev. Moon asked the right question when he read the Bible, even though he was crying. (laughter). But I just want to point out, in his context there would have been a lot of people reading the Bible to find out, "What shall I do to be saved?" Consequently, you read the Bible to find what's in it for you. But that wasn't Moon's question when he read the Bible. Nor do I think that Rev. Moon read the Bible from the perspective of "What is God trying to say to us in the Bible." That is already much too propositional. And I've never heard, until you said that, any Unification person speak that way, suggesting that the Bible is God talking. I think Rev. Moon read the Bible saying, "What is God's purpose? What is the purpose of God in all this?" Which is to say that you don't have in the Unification Church any doctrine of the Bible being the infallible, totally accurate word of God, in that sense. But you have, as a hermeneutical question behind Unification theology, "What is the purpose of God in creation?" It's trying to read the biblical record as a kind of access to the will and purpose of God. What was God trying to do in the world? There's still another way to read it, and I have a certain affection for this one, being an old Calvinist. One might read it asking, "How does this record reveal to us, or manifest to us and testify to us, the glory of God?" This approach is somewhat more theocentric but still I think that there's an orientation to the purpose of God in creation that is behind Rev. Moon's reading of the Bible. That, then, leads to all kinds of texts becoming meaningful.

Jonathan Wells: Calvin starts his *Institutes* by talking about piety, right? That's his starting point, and that's why I talked about Rev. Moon's tears because that's a kind of piety. But now the hermeneutical question — I think there are two issues here. One is how he arrived at what he calls an interpretation of the Scripture, and the other is how we evaluate it. I think the two are very closely connected. But certainly in a formal sense we have to distinguish the two. I don't think that Rev. Moon has to know Christian theological history to arrive at his interpretation.

Theologian X: What do you mean, "Has to know?" In a sense, obviously it's true that he didn't have to know.

Jonathan Wells: I don't think he actually did know, though I don't know that for sure.

Theologian X: By "has to know," do you mean it would not have been desirable that he know?

Jonathan Wells: I think that where the theological tradition comes in is in the evaluation of what he's saying. Certainly we want to take the *Divine Principle* and compare it with the Council of Nicea and the christological disputes and find out where it stands in relation to those issues. Does it enlighten the dispute? Does it clarify questions that have been unclarified? Now, that to me is the fascinating question and that's why I'm studying theology. I think as the day goes on, some of these issues will be specifically discussed. I think, in fact, that's our job. Our theological job is to take a proposal like the *Divine Principle* and evaluate it. I think we can take it and analyze it theologically. Does it clarify serious and deep problems in the Bible itself and in the Western Christian tradition?

Darrol Bryant: I'm going to let Virginia state her question, and come back to Mr. X, just to get the questions on the floor, and then we'll take a short break.

Virginia Hearn: This is not a question so much as a response. Durwood referred to the centuries of Christian tradition that those working in theology now are familiar with and work from. It seems to me that we have to recognize that the Western tradition of Christianity and the Eastern, too, for that matter, have been in the hands of males who had a certain role in their given culture. Now, whenever you have a socio-cultural group other than the white male come to the Bible and take it seriously, it is inevitable that they are going to pick up different things. They are going to have different sensitivities. They are going to find different points relevant to their own situation. We have another example of this today in the case of a little handful of what are called biblical feminists in this country. We take the Scripture seriously, and we are knowledgeable of traditional interpretations. But at the same time we recognize that when we study, when we exposit, when we translate, we at times see things differently. We see different points to emphasize. We have some fresh understandings that then become important to us. So if we were to come up with a systematic theology of our own, I have no doubt that there would be some different thrusts. It's easy for the traditional white male establishment to look at that and give it a quick putdown and say it's heretical. Maybe it is, and maybe it isn't. It may be just a different pair of spectacles.

Darrol Bryant: That's an important observation, Virginia.

Theologian X: I think there's more than a hermeneutical question at stake in Jonathan's comment. What Jonathan said surprised me a bit. Why? Well, because hermeneutics, as I read the discussion of the last century and a half, is a principle for understanding how we interpret an ancient text without any reference to the supernatural intervention of God. From that point of view, we might look at Rev. Moon's interpretation of the Scripture which, according to Jonathan, is the result of Rev. Moon's reading the Bible many times in an attempt to discern what it is that God Himself wants. But — and here's the problem — that doesn't square with what I understand is Rev. Moon's own claim, namely that this is a new revelation. This is not an interpretation of an old revelation, but a new one. He describes his own view as absolutely new, totally fresh. The *Divine Principle* is a new revelation. It's not a re-application of the old one. Speaking on behalf of evangelical Christianity, the problem of the modern world is not a problem of revelation, it's the problem of sin. A new revelation is not going to cure that one. The old revelation was definitive, it was a complete enough expression of who God is. People just choose, understanding the truth, to disobey God. It seems to me that the problem of sin cannot be cured with any new revealed truth. So there are two issues: one, the false presupposition, I think, that a new revelation will relieve the problems of the modern world — I think that's intellectually weak — and then, secondly, that which really in terms of our tradition makes Unification theology heretical, namely, that it feels it necessary to add to and supplement the revelation which the Christian church has deemed to be an already completed one.

Holly Sherman: I'd just like to say one thing. Earlier Professor Richardson was saying that Rev. Moon asked the right question when he read the Bible. I agree that Rev. Moon didn't go to the Bible saying, "How can I be saved?" I also don't think he was trying to find some truth, or even that his question was about God's purpose of creation. I believe that when Rev. Moon was young he had a fairly good life, but that he began to realize at some point that mankind was really suffering. For some reason, he felt so strongly that he wanted to find a way to end that suffering. Along with that, he thought that if God is the Creator of man, if God is the Father of man, then He also must be suffering very much. It is at this point that Rev. Moon began to pray really seriously, and really ask God, "Why? Where did this suffering come from? Where did this evilness come from?" His desire was to find out where it came from so that he could find a way to end it. This is also what guided his study of the Bible, his searching to find out where evil came from, and how in history God has been working with man to end evil and suffering. That, I think, is where the *Divine Principle* comes from.

Darrol Bryant: You've helped clarify something that for me has been disturbing about the Unification Church, and that is that it is such a terribly monolithic group. (laughter) We've now had at least six different readings of the *Divine Principle,* its origins, its central purposes, its central questions. (laughter) Let's take a five-minute break.

Hermeneutics: The Divine Principle and Scripture

Darrol Bryant: I have a request. The request is for a simple and short statement from the members of the Unification Church about what the *Divine Principle* is. I warned the asker of this question that I doubted that we could get a short and simple answer to the question. Nonetheless, I thought it important to make sure that everyone is fairly comfortable that they have some rough idea of what the *Divine Principle* is. In this way we can talk about these problems on the foundation of some understanding of what the substance of this theological position is.

Yoshihiko Masuda: Do you mean the *Divine Principle* book or...

Darrol Bryant: That's the question that I was asking you: What do *you* mean by the "Divine Principle?" Do you mean this book or something that is in this book or a cosmic principle, or what?

Dagfinn Aslid: If you ask what the "Divine Principle" is, you'll get at least six different answers. I understand the Divine Principle as revelation, but I have to tell you what revelation means. I would be tempted to draw a parallel here with Pannenberg's notion of revelation as history. The *Divine Principle* is not something out of a bottle or something completely broken off from the rest of history. I see it as very much in touch with history and tradition. When we in the Unification Church speak of revelation, we speak about progressive revelation and stages in revelation where new revelation is based on prior revelations, yet transforming them and expanding them. In this perspective, I'd call the *Divine Principle* a continuing attempt to articulate the most comprehensive tradition. As concerns history, we try to overcome the split between "Historie" (history as facts) and "Geschichte" (history as meaning) which has become a problem. Some people have been asking about the relationship between Rev. Moon and the Christian tradition. I think the attempt in the *Divine Principle* is explicitly not to isolate the Christian tradition, but to aim towards a universal history and articulate a Christian theology in that perspective. This is very explicit in our historiology: specifically Christian history is central to universal history. I think the *Divine Principle* needs to be understood as an historical perspective in that sense. I would stress the developing and open-ended character of the *Divine Principle*. It is giving us an ever-expanding and more comprehensive horizon. That is how I understand it.

Yoshihiko Masuda: I'd like to go back to the text. First of all, the *Divine Principle* is the interpretation in English of the original title of the book in Korean or Japanese. The original title of the book is not *Divine Principle*. The literal translation of the title in Japanese and Korean is *Discourses on Principle.*

Darrol Bryant: Principle in the singular or plural?

Yoshihiko Masuda: There are no articles to distinguish singular or plural in Korean and Japanese.

Durwood Foster: Mr. Kim feels it should be plural. We were just talking about the same thing during the break. But you're saying there's no difference.

Yoshihiko Masuda: It's not so clear in the original Korean language, because in Korean and Japanese, there's usually no difference in form between plural and singular. It's unspecified in the original Korean language. When I joined the Unification Church I studied an earlier edition of the *Divine Principle*. The literal translation of the title of that book was *Elucidation of Principle* or *Explanation of Principle*. The new edition is *Discourses on Principle*. That's the English translation of the Japanese title. We don't use the term "Divine Principle" in Japanese when we discuss Unification theology. We use "Unification Principle," not "Divine Principle."

Theologian X: Do you think it's a mistake to use the adjective "divine"?

Yoshihiko Masuda: My personal preference is the literal translation, *Discourses on Principle.*

Theologian X: But why do you prefer that? What is your motive for being particularly resistant to the word "divine"?

Yoshihiko Masuda: In English discussion there is always a confusion between the *Divine Principle* book and the Principle itself. In Japanese and Korean, there's no confusion between the textbook, *Discourses on Principle,* and the Unification Principle. So, personally, I prefer the title *Discourses on Principle.*

Patricia Zulkosky: Actually, as I understand it, the title *Divine Principle* was given to the book by a western missionary who had gone to Korea. They were discussing what it should be titled and this missionary who was studying our movement at that time, came up with the title, *Divine Principle.* So that became the English title. It didn't come from Rev. Moon.

Stillson Judah: I would like to make an observation concerning a trend I observe in the movement. It seems to me that this is an example of a very perceptible trend towards diminishing the divine or absolute claim that is being made for the book. Earlier on, the text of the *Divine Principle* seemed to have an aura about it of a new revelation comparable to the Old and New Testament. But recently, and today particularly, it seems to me the tenor of the comments is to say: "Don't make the mistake of thinking we're absolutizing this book. It's not divine, it's a discourse on Principle. Or it's an open-ended search to unify the human vision of truth, or something like that." So there's a kind of debunking or iconoclastic trend that would disabuse us of thinking that there is any kind of idolatry associated with this book. I see that as compatible with the efforts that I understand to be under way now to revise it or to redact it in some way. I don't see that trend as in any way demeaning. I welcome this. I can see that it corresponds to inner felt needs in the movement, but I just wonder if I'm right in this perception. Would anyone like to contradict what I'm saying?

Anthony Guerra: I don't want to contradict it at all. I think, however, that that same kind of debunking is also part of our approach to the Old and New Testaments. That is, that we don't really propositionalize revelation. The Old Testament and the New Testament are looked on as textbooks of truth, rather than the truth itself.

Yoshihiko Masuda: I want to add some points concerning my understanding or interpretation of Divine Principle. In Japanese, there is no equivalent word to "Divine Principle." In Japanese we say Unification Principle, or just Principle. In my understanding of the Principle, with a capital letter, it is truth, invisible, but absolute, unchangeable, eternal. The *Divine Principle* book is an attempt to express that invisible, absolute, eternal Principle. The *Divine Principle* book is not absolute, but an expression of truth, an expression of the Principle. So I can see the eventuality of some revision, adding or changing the *Divine Principle* book itself. The *Divine Principle* book is a new interpretation of the Bible. The Bible is also an expression of the Principle, the eternal, absolute principle.

Darrol Bryant: Could you comment on the term "revelation"? Do you know anything about the Korean word that is translated into English as "revelation"?

Yoshihiko Masuda: Yes, I know the equivalent word. I think it has the same common sense meaning as in English.

Darrol Bryant: What would you understand the common sense meaning of "revelation" to be?

Yoshihiko Masuda: I don't see a difference between the English and Korean word.

Darrol Bryant: OK, and what do you understand by the English word "revelation"?

Yoshihiko Masuda: Something given by God.

Durwood Foster: Is "revelation" a word in Korean or Japanese that only came into vogue through contact with Christianity? Or was the same word in the vocabulary before?

Yoshihiko Masuda: It came from Christian theology.

Herbert Richardson: "Given by God," of course, is the technical definition for grace, not revelation. Everything is grace: interpretation can be a grace, revelation can be a grace, a meal that you eat is a grace. So, if that's the case, you can't place very much on somebody saying, "Well, I've got a new revelation." It just means, "I've been given a new grace in my life."

Dagfinn Aslid: I'd just like to make a distinction between a supernaturalist conception of revelation, and a more rational understanding of revelation. I mentioned earlier that I draw a parallel between Pannenberg's notion of revelation which tends to be a view of God as revealed in history and creation and our view. I think that our notion of revelation tends towards that rationalistic side, rather than supernatural.

Theologian X: I haven't read everything, but in Young Oon Kim's interpretation of the *Divine Principle,** she's clearly a

---

*Young Oon Kim, *Divine Principle and its Application,* various editions, Washington D.C.: Holy Spirit Association for the Unification of World Christianity, 1960-1972.

supernaturalist. Do you find yourself in tune with her interpretation?

Dagfinn Aslid: Why is she a supernaturalist?

Theologian X: Her world view includes a variety of spirits that persist beyond death, who press themselves into the lives of other people who are living physically. That is clearly one symptom of a supernaturalist world view, and I would see that as quite different from the concept of reality as historical that you find in Pannenberg.

Dagfinn Aslid: I'd like to make two comments. First of all, Unification wants to embrace the different paths or styles or modes of knowledge. It is almost like the Jungian cross of cognition: the way of the intellect, the emotions, the will, and the intuition. We too affirm these different modes of knowing. Secondly, this diversity can be seen in the diversity of its spiritualities. Our movement is more charismatic in England where I was working last summer. The whole English family is very different from the German family. That is partly a function of the style of leadership. I find the English family to be much more—if we might use the word—supernatural, or I would say, spiritual in its orientation. Whereas the German family is much more centered on rationality and clarity in order to move ahead with a lot of energy and efficiency. In that sense, our movement isn't very monolithic. Now if we were to speak epistemologically of our view of what we call the spirit world and spirits, I think we tend to include that as rational. We tend to speak about spirits — if I may use the word — scientifically, but I'm not saying that in a constrictive sense.

Durwood Foster: I'd like to comment on that very briefly. I appreciate this effort to explicate the mode in which revelation is understood to have occurred in the *Divine Principle* and through Rev. Moon. But it seems to me, in point of fact, that what you're saying is very problematic. It seems to me that there is something quite specifically supernatural in Rev. Moon's reception of his new vision or insight or code for interpreting the Bible. It is one that would stand in blatant contrast with the normal meaning of the word "rational" which would be something accessible to the human intellect in general. Earlier, in a private conversation, Mr. Kim was emphasizing — and this has seemed to me to generally be the case in Unification self-understanding — that what happened in the case of Rev. Moon was something exceedingly particular and discontinuous with general, rational cognition. It's not something that could be recapitulated or publicly demonstrated. Rather it goes back to the event that occurred when he was 16 years old, and continues from that point to the actual writing of the *Divine Principle*. There is something very, very different from what Pannenberg proposes going on. What Rev. Moon comes up with is not something that is subject to a general, rational demonstration, at least it has not been ordinarily understood as such.

Dagfinn Aslid: However, it's in the style of theologizing that I would say it's similar to Pannenberg. When, for example, Pannenberg speaks about revelation as an historical event without finality he is very close to our view. He then affirms the historical critical method and the rational approach to history. In a similar way, we would affirm an occurrence of spiritual communication as something that is completely explained in our ontology. In the case of Rev. Moon, the revelation which he had was painstakingly worked out for years and then explicated and made rational in a way that is plain for all to see.

Herbert Richardson: I have a comment on what you're saying and also a general question on the Principle. Is it or isn't it a new revelation? The argument, it seems to me, runs a little like this. In a sense the question is not whether there is a teaching which is a new revelation to go alongside the Bible. In a sense the question is really this: has God continued to work in history in a salvific way since the time of the apostles? Or is it the case that, as practically all Protestants believe in their denial of tradition, that God has not done anything salvific in history since the time of the apostles? Ever since the time of the apostles, we live by faith in Jesus Christ, awaiting His return. History is totally the sphere of mankind. There is nothing that has occurred in history that comes from God, in God's pursuing His purpose. We just live by faith in this blind, dark world. That's the Protestant position. The Protestant interpretation of the history of the Christian church is that it is the history of the deformation of the true Christian Gospel by human beings until the true Gospel was recovered by a couple of people, Luther and Calvin. I personally think that tradition is totally nonsensical. The Catholics are absolutely right. Why are they right? The Catholics understand that God has continued to work salvifically in history since the time of the apostles. And our knowledge of that ushers in the claim that there are two sources of revelation: Scripture and tradition. The question, however, is not whether there are two sources of revelation, Scripture and tradition. But the question that every Protestant has to face is, "Are you really willing to live with the consequence of your claim that Scripture alone is the sole revelation? The consequence is that you deny that God has continued to work salvifically in history ever since the time of Jesus Christ, except for saving souls for the other world." Now, I think that Protestantism is, quite frankly, blind to the grace and purposes of God.

Durwood Foster: I have a lot of sympathy with the thrust of your comment. Yet I feel it is a caricature of the Protestant position, or at least an extremely truncated statement of it. Even the classical Protestant position which most approximates what you're saying does, I think, rest on the premise that in great figures like Luther and Calvin, in the reformers, and in my own special tradition, John Wesley, God continues to be active, through the principle of interpretation by the internal testimony of the Holy Spirit, conjoined with the canonical authority of the Bible. There is positively the notion that God continues to be salvifically active, not only in the saving of souls, but in the shaping of historical destiny, the reform of the church, the correction of the perversion of Christian truth that occurred in the Catholic Church and so on. In addition to this stream we're talking about, there is the whole enthusiast tradition, the people who rely on the new outpouring of the Spirit in a way that emphasizes, even more than Catholicism does, that God continues to break into history revealingly. Then, too, there's the whole liberal development in Protestantism, which is in some ways the reverse of classical Protestantism because it identifies the progressive evolution of history as God's continuing salvific operation. Your statement, as I know you would acknowledge, is not really adequate to Protestantism as a whole. I just say that by way of a footnote, because with your positive position, I'm very much in sympathy.

Herbert Richardson: But it's intended as a kind of polemical gambit. And it's good in a sense, as a move against those in the Protestant world who would want to argue a "sola scriptura" position. While I don't think that the book is a revelation, I think that there is a revelational work of God in history since the time of the apostles up to the present. But why can't the Unification Church have this tradition and still be Christian? Or to put it in another way, if the Moonies can't, is the whole of Rome wrong also? And, of course, the very worst example in the Protestant world, I think — and I say this with deep love — is Luther. I'm sure that there is no human being in Western history whose name is quoted as an authority more than Luther. I mean, Luther, Luther, Luther, by the people who claim that the only authority is "sola scriptura." (laughter.)

Theologian X: I think I'm in sympathy with the direction in which you are going, but I think I would have formulated it slightly differently. I don't see the problem created by "sola scriptura" over against God's continuing salvific work. The problem that "sola scriptura" raises is one of authority in revelation, which I think is a quite different issue from the one you raised. One can acknowledge that God continues to work day in and day out, but "sola scriptura" has to do with the authority of revelation. I don't think it speaks to whether or not God's saving work has stopped or whether it continues.

Herbert Richardson: You don't think so? I think it does, in fact. And I think that it has functioned that way in Protestant history. The Protestants have used "sola scriptura" against the Catholic doctrine of "scriptura et traditio."

Theologian X: Yes, I understand that, but I just don't see how soteriology is at stake there.

Durwood Foster: I think that the relationship is that the authority helps you to judge what actions in history are really God's actions. Maybe you can say that the Protestants have chosen "sola scriptura" because there's a lot of confusion and if you have only one Scripture, that cleans things up.

Herbert Richardson: I think the basic point is that the Unification Church is trying to discern the continuing and developing work of God in history in relation to the project of God's purpose, namely, salvation. Therefore, it is not just concerned about *more* revelation, but is concerned about *more* salvation! It's concern is to give to the life of the Church a holy history which doesn't, like Cullmann's, come to an end at the time of Jesus. Rather, Unification comes right up to the present, and offers, not a theology in the old sense, but a philosophy or theology of history. I think the question is now, how do we judge that question?

Jonathan Wells: You will admit there will be competing theologies of history?

Herbert Richardson: Sure.

Darrol Bryant: That goes back to Jonathan's question but now it's shifted over to the area of evaluation. That's an important shift since it suggests that the problem is not that some followers of Rev. Moon have written the *Divine Principle,* but that the problem is whether or not these things that are written down in this text are true. What are the norms by which one would proceed towards that evaluation?

Theologian X: I think that may relate to the authority issue.

Darrol Bryant: It does relate to the authority issue, but it's a question that's a general question that relates to the evaluation of any proposal as to what we within the Christian tradition should believe.

Theologian X: I would say that there are some dramatically new things in the *Divine Principle.* I don't claim to be an expert on it, but there is in my judgment a distinctively different interpretation of the fall, and in that sense, then, of the human problem. Therefore, there is also a distinctively different proposal as to how the human problem is to be rectified. It is one that is in continuity with, and builds upon, the other preceding traditions, to be sure, but it's also distinctively different. And then on the basis of all of that, there is the suggestion or the anticipation that the fulfillment of this needed rectification is about to occur. Indeed, there is a strong hint that it is already taking place if we could only see, or at least that we may hopefully expect that confirmation may soon occur since the bringer of this rectification is among us. All of those things, I would say, if true, or whether true or not, are distinctively different from the older tradition. If they are true, it is a new revelation, I would say.

Darrol Bryant: Would you clarify that term you used, "new revelation." You mean it's a new disclosure of God, is that how you would use it?

Theologian X: Yes, I would mean it that way. It claims to be a distinctive, new disclosure of the truth of God for human life. A decisive, new disclosure would, for me, merit the term "revelation." Of course, like any other word, it's subject to interpretation.

Jonathan Wells: I thought that our view of the fall was part of the whole tradition. If you read St. Augustine and the *City of God,* he says that human sexuality became disordered through the fall and through the disorder of human sexuality, sin is transmitted from generation to generation. I think that that story is repeated so many times, it is so well understood, that in the popular mind people who aren't even Christian will tell you that's what Christians believe. The popular view is that Christians

believe that sex is bad because Adam and Eve sinned, and they
were ashamed, and so forth. The Unification view, our story of
how the fall took place, far from being something new is, at least
in the popular mind, very familiar. It's the theologians who don't
believe it anymore! Why? Well, it's because they've developed
another idea that in relation to the orthodox tradition is heterodox. We've heard so many times that sex is "just natural," that
theologians may actually think that the Unification proposal is
novel. But it seems to me that it's close to old orthodoxy.

Theologian X: I think that it's wholesome that you are
pinpointing this issue, because it does suggest that we might
inquire very specifically into the understanding of the fall in the
Divine Principle and in subsequent Unification interpretation.
I've already said that I don't claim to be an expert on it, but I've
had the impression that you hold the view that some sort of
sexual pollution or contamination took place in which the satanic
principle got in on the act and polluted or contaminated what
would otherwise have been the pure and good fulfillment of
God's purpose. And, Jesus would have rectified that had He had
time to get around to it but didn't, and now it needs to be made
up. This, of course is not the whole story, but that seems to be a
specific motif that is divergent from the main line of the classical
Christian tradition. But, as I say, that's something that we need to
pinpoint and to go into specifically. I wouldn't want the whole
weight of what I was saying about novelty a moment ago to rest
on this one point. I just mentioned that as one of three main
things that I gave as illustrations, and the latter two are perhaps
more decisive, really, than that first one.

Jonathan Wells: I'd like to talk about the fall if we have time.

Darrol Bryant: We don't have time now, but I would suggest
that that be the topic that we begin with after lunch.

Jonathan Wells: I just wanted to continue my preface and
point out that when I do talk about it, I think I can illustrate this
question of validation. That is, we're taking a theological proposal
like the *Divine Principle* and correlating it with Scripture and the
Christian tradition, and finding out if it's faithful to the essential
meaning of Scripture and tradition, and at the same time perhaps
novel. That's what I'll try to do when I get around to doing it.

Stillson Judah: I'm trying to sort all of this out in my own
mind, and one of the things that bothers me is this: if the *Divine
Principle* can be said to be a new disclosure of truth from God in

any sense of the word, then it seems to me at that point that you have a new revelation. The point I'm very interested in is the question of how this differs, we might say, from Islam. There we have a view which says, "Yes, we recognize the Old Testament as one of *the* books, we recognize the position of Jesus, the New Testament is one of *the* books. But resting on this tradition, we have a new disclosure of truth, through Mohammed, which is now called the Koran." I'm continually bothered by this because I hear something here that seems to me is very close to the analogy between the Old Testament, Judaism and Christianity versus the Koran or a new revelation in Islam. Now, how is this different?

Dagfinn Aslid: Very briefly: I see the *Divine Principle* as something that makes a greater effort at correlation and continuity with Scripture. The Koran tends, systematically speaking, to stand more distinct from the Old and New Testament. I think the effort at synthesis is more explicit and central in the Principle.

Richard Quebedeaux: This brings up a theory that a friend of mine has and I think it's correct. Unification is a new religious movement out of which has come this text called the *Divine Principle.* But how is this movement to be interpreted? It can be interpreted, on the one hand, as a new religion with a new revelation. It can also be interpreted, on the other hand, as a renewal movement within Christianity with a new interpretation of Scripture. Now, the question is how is it going to develop? What's going to happen to Unification? If, on the one hand, it is isolated from the other Christian traditions, it will invariably lead to the elevation of the *Divine Principle,* especially after Rev. Moon dies, to the point where it becomes like the *Book of Mormon,* almost canonical. The other possible direction, and I think I've already seen some evidence for this development, is that in conversation with other Christians, Unification will come to appreciate the centrality of Scripture and Christ more than it seems to do now.

Consequently, you will want to talk about the *Divine Principle* more as an interpretation of Scripture, a work which for Unificationists is like Calvin's *Institutes* is to orthodox Calvinists. I think one of the critical things affecting the route Unification will take is the intellectual dialogue that's going on at every level. I think that if the *Divine Principle* ever becomes canonical, and in fact co-equal with Scripture, that would be the end of ecumenical discussion. We have a parallel in the development of the Church of the New Jerusalem, the Swedenborgians, a small intellectual sect that has two strands. One strand uses Swedenborg's writings as an interpretation of Scripture, but not co-equal to Scripture and not revelatory in the sense that Scripture is. This is the main-line Swedenborgians who are now members of the National Council of Churches. Even though their theology is very, very different from main-line Christendom, it has not elevated the writings of Swedenborg to equality with Scripture. Whereas there is the split-off group of equal size which makes the writings of Swedenborg co-equal to Scripture as a new revelation, and they are totally sectarian.

I know some people at Barrytown who would like Unificationism to be like Mormonism, really. And then there's a very strong and emerging conflict with those who are very much more akin to the main-line historic Christian traditions, who state that, "If *Divine Principle* ever becomes canonical, I'm going to leave the movement."

Virginia Hearn: Recognizing the truth of Jonathan's claim that in the popular mind there is a sexual connotation to the fall, I am not convinced that this is in Augustine. I've never been aware that this was in Augustine.

Jonathan Wells: I will send you a couple of texts —

Virginia Hearn: And of course I will immediately say that Augustine isn't necessarily authoritative.

Jonathan Wells: The question is whether or not it's in the tradition. Actually I think that the tradition of understanding the fall as sexual comes into Christianity from Judaism. It would be marvelous to have a good biblical scholar here. But in all honesty is it really the case that nobody had ever heard, until they heard from Rev. Moon, that sin entered the world by Satan or a serpent seducing Eve and having a sexual relation?

Durwood Foster: That's not exactly to the point. I mean, everything that Jesus said was anticipated in the inter-testamental or Old Testament literature. It does not in any way refute the revelatory character of a revelation that the motifs or thematic elements in it have been in existence prior to it.

Darrrol Bryant: I agree totally on that point, Durwood, and that's why I'm still unclear about what exactly the question is about this being a new revelation. I have trouble understanding what that question is for precisely that reason. As I read the *Divine Principle,* I say, "Yes, it's put together in a kind of novel way, there are some new things here," but are these different in *kind* from what we see in any other text? To say in an absolute way that there's something new here doesn't make any sense to me. I don't think it makes any sense to speak about the Scripture in that way either.

Theologian X: Maybe revelation is a word you can't use.

Darrol Bryant: No, I do use it in the first sense that you mentioned, that in the Scripture God is disclosed. I believe that. I accept that. But the corollary is not that God is not disclosed anywhere else.

Herbert Richardson: The technical problem is the *definiens,* the distinguishing mark of revelation. Is that *definiens* that it be new? It seems to me that what Durwood is saying is that the *definiens* of revelation is not that it be new, but that it be from God. Just to give you an example, Calvin argued that the teaching of the New Testament was exactly like the teaching of the Old Testament. The difference was not newness, but just order, a dispensation appropriate to the time and age. What makes it revelation? That it's from God, that it's binding, is Calvin's view.

Well, then, with Unification, maybe the interesting question is not whether or not the doctrine that they teach is new, but on what grounds — this is very Catholic — is it authoritative? Is it authoritative because it's taught by Rev. Moon? Or is it authoritative because it is taught by Scripture? Or is it authoritative because Rev. Moon, on the basis of the authority of Scripture, presents a true interpretation of Scripture to us? I think, by the way, Catholics often say this: "OK, you're right, but you may be wrong if the reason that you're right is the wrong reason." So we want to know, "Do you believe this by faith and trust in the teaching of the magisterial office of the Church, or do you believe this by your own reason?" Some things Catholics are obliged to believe on the basis of the teaching of the magisterium, and other things they're obliged to believe on the basis of the capacity of reason. Now we're clearly into the problem of revelation as the mode of authorization of the knowledge that you have, not the content, whether it's new or not. That's clearly a whole different way to pose it, and much closer, I think, to where the question lies.

Durwood Foster: I think so too, and what you're saying is illuminating and, I think, sound. But I would say in addition that there are *some* aspects of newness in the facticity or givenness of a revelation. I was simply suggesting that they do not stand or fall with the novelty of the thematic elements or motifs that come together in the new revelation. I do think that there is in a new revelation a novel coalescence or synthesis of the elements. But that is compatible with, and I would want to subjoin it to what you were saying about the mode of authority. I think that's involved and that's what gives the new coalescence or synthesis its thrust or decisiveness. It is that part of the whole dynamic that has sometimes been called the work of the Holy Spirit. That can't be left out in the total diagnosis of what is involved in what we called revelation — though there's also this other aspect of novelty that cannot be ignored either.

Anthony Guerra: In many ways that's how I view what Rev. Moon did. He had all of the elements of the *Divine Principle* given in Scripture: the creation, the story of the fall, Christ, salvation, eschatology, the Second Coming. Through his reading of the Scripture — much like the reformers under the inspiration of the Holy Spirit—he coalesced these things into a new synthesis, which is written in this book we call the *Divine Principle.*

I think the difference between the Koran and the *Divine Principle* has to do with the way in which the person of Christ, not the Scripture, but the way in which the person of Christ, the reality of Christ, is dealt with. That is, in the Koran, the messianic office, the singular nature of the person of Jesus as the Messiah is denied, whereas in the *Divine Principle* it's upheld. For the *Divine Principle* Jesus is the Messiah, unlike other prophets. That statement is explicitly made. It seems to me that's the point where we stand in differentiation from Islam, or other religions; this point places us within the Christian tradition.

Theologian X: How about the Old Testament and the New Testament? We have an Old Testament which represents an older revelation, we have a New Testament which represents a new revelation which is based, of course, on the Old Testament. But now, can we not say that the revelation in the *Divine Principle* rests also on the Old Testament as well as the New Testament, and it is also a new revelation in the same way that the New Testament is a new revelation in relation to the Old Testament?

Anthony Guerra: But you see, the question we're raising concerns the meaning of revelation. If we take the definition that we've talked about, as a kind of coalescence of given elements, then I would say that for some Christians the Old Testament is...

Theologian X: I think Stillson Judah's question stands as

asked. It doesn't depend on the definition of revelation, it depends upon the authority status it holds within the tradition: how canonical is it? I think that without even defining revelation, the question is still a fair one.

Anthony Guerra: I think it is, but I think that Richard Quebedeaux has partly suggested the context for the appropriation of that question, and that is, that it very much depends on what happens between now and Rev. Moon's death and how other traditions respond to this movement.

Herbert Richardson: That's why a theological conference like this is not just concerned with understanding the Unification movement but is also working to try to push the movement in one direction or the other. People like myself are eager to work to hold the Unification movement within the Christian tradition and to strengthen that attachment. Other people, by attacking the Church, are trying to push it outside in a sectarian way. It seems to me that theologians play, especially in respect to this movement, a very important formative role in determining the future of the Unification Church in relation to Christian tradition. It's a real challenge to us, because it seems to me that the Unification movement raises the question of the Western character of Christianity. Here we encounter an indigenous form of orientalized Christianity. What are we going to do with it? And even more it raises the problem of the Christian tradition in relation to the world religions. All these questions are at stake here.

Interpreting Creation and Fall

Darrol Bryant: I think we may begin again. This afternoon we will begin by letting Pat say a couple of things about the doctrine of creation and the three blessings. Then we're going to let Jonathan, who is sitting there with his manuscript by his side (laughter), say some things about the fall. He has that worked out and he is going to read to us. (laughter)

That will probably take us until coffee time, and then after that, we'll spend the rest of the afternoon on eschatology and hermeneutics. Anthony is going to say something about that topic to introduce it. We will do this against the backdrop of the hermeneutical discussion and with an eye to the practice of the Church. If we try to relate these doctrines to the way in which Unification organizes its life and incarnates these doctrinal formulations then we will get an additional angle on our whole discussion. That will take us through the afternoon. We're invited this evening to the Dursts' where we will have supper, and after supper there will be a conversation on the things that are still on people's minds. Pat, would you like to begin?

Patricia Zulkosky: The question, as Dr. Richardson argued, that Rev. Moon is asking is, "What is the purpose of creation and man's life?" We believe that we can arrive at some understanding of God by looking at the nature of man, in an ideal sense, and creation. Through this kind of process, we come to the conclusion that God has both masculine and feminine natures, internal and external aspects, and a number of other complementary aspects. We know that God, having all of these different attributes, can in and of Himself have relationship, in a sense, inside Himself. Man can also have give-and-take inside himself with, for instance, the idea of chocolate cake, but until that becomes a substantial reality that a person can have give-and-take with in a more substantial way, there's something lacking. So in the same way, God could conceive of the blueprint of the creation of children who would be responsive to His nature. But unless this became a living reality, there would be something lacking in the joy that God could feel.

From the beginning, God conceived of an *ideal* blue-print, not of a creation that would be deformed or full of suffering and struggle. This ideal we feel is summarized in the Scripture in three words, when God tells man to be fruitful, to multiply, and to have dominion. These three aspects of life are what we call the three blessings. The first blessing involves centering our lives on God. Man is to completely unite mind and body centering on God and the direction of goodness. The result of this would be what we call a man or woman of perfect personality. God created man so that each person could have grown in maturity to be the visible reflection of a unique aspect of God. Each person has that responsibility to become an object to God in a very real way. If even one person fails to do that, then there's some aspect of God that can't be completely fulfilled. So ultimately, every human being needs to fulfill his or her unique potential. Sometimes, in fulfilling the first blessing, you will hear people saying that this is the meaning of becoming perfect. For us, perfect doesn't mean climbing to the top of a mountain as an end point from which you can't go any further. But it's the point of maturation where the possiblities for man to fulfill his uniqueness are opened up. A tiny baby can't pick up a straight pin and put it in a pop bottle. It's impossible. You need a certain amount of maturation on all different levels in order to be able to do those things. For us, perfection isn't the end point, but it's the beginning point of man's development and fulfillment of his individual uniqueness.

Even so, just one person, one man who becomes this man of perfect personality would only be the expression of the masculine nature of God, and as such, couldn't understand the depths of the feminine nature of God. In a similar way, an ideal woman couldn't understand the male nature of God. So it takes man and woman together, acting as a unit, to really experience the fullness of the nature of God. This is the second blessing. Also through the procreative act and having children, they can in a sense stand in the position of God to their children. Adam and Eve were born without sin, and had the responsibility to grow to reach maturity or perfection. Then as sinless expressions of the nature of God, they could have given birth to sinless, but still immature children, who also would have had to grow. But these children would have had the advantage of perfect parents, ideal parents, to raise them. God becomes, not only the parental God, but He's a grandparent, and this whole kind of familial situation develops.

Then the third blessing is to take dominion over creation, so that, after man has developed his heart and relationship to God, and his ability to love mankind, he can take this same heart and apply it to creation, being very sensitive to the purpose of creation as God's way of giving joy to man. Through man, creation can fulfill its purpose and give joy to God. Through our sensitivity and our relationship to creation, we can extend a great deal of joy and satisfaction to creation. Creation's ability to serve man and be appreciated for its service to man can return so much joy and stimulation back to God. Man stands in the mediator position between God and the rest of creation. These are the three blessings.

Another point that's very important in our idea of creation is the idea that man has a physical man and also a spiritual man. Our physical man has five senses with which we can perceive the physical world, and it needs certain things in order to grow like air and sunlight, food and water. At the same time that man is conceived and born, his spirit man is also created. Our spirit man also has five senses. We can understand in this sense terms like clairvoyance and clairaudience. Ideally speaking, if man hadn't fallen, we would be fully aware of our spiritual senses and be able to perceive the spiritual world freely at will. It may be something like tuning in a different station on the radio or television. Birth would be a very major celebration in the life of man, as the beginning of our physical life and also the beginning of our eternal life. Then marriage, of course, would be a second celebration for man, and death would be a third. Because man is made of the same elements as the rest of physical creation and the rest of physical creation has a life and death cycle, we believe that our physical man also has a life and death cycle. But our spirit man has, we believe, an eternal existence. Just as our physical man needs certain things to grow, our spirit man also needs certain things to grow. Parallel to sun and air for our physical man would be God's truth and love. Parallel to those things like food and water that man has to make an effort to get would be man's good deeds, and by doing good deeds, our spirit man is nourished by what we call vitality elements. It's through our time on earth that we grow our spirit man through realizing the three blessings as well as our physical self to the point where we can be an expression of the nature of God. For us, physical death is a natural occurrence, and yet we also have eternal life in the spiritual world with our spirit man. I think these are the basic points that Jonathan can build on.

Jonathan Wells: I'm just going to go through a quick summary of the Unification doctrine of the fall. There are two starting points for what I'm going to say. One is in Genesis where we have the story of Adam and Eve being told by God not to eat of the tree of knowledge of good and evil. The serpent conversed with Eve, deceived her, and she ate the fruit, and she went to Adam and he did likewise. God then evicted them from the Garden of Eden. The other element is the philosophical one, probably as old as Genesis, certainly as old as the Old Testament, and that is, "What is the origin of evil?" Christian traditions, against which the new theological proposals in the *Divine Principle* have to be measured, have always used this Adam and Eve story as the explanation for the origin of evil. The key issue is this: God is good, but there's evil in the world. God, being good, couldn't create the evil. Where did the evil come from? The traditional answer is that evil is grounded in human free will. Mankind has free will, and freely chose to turn away from God. This happened in the Garden of Eden with Adam and Eve.

The Genesis story by itself, of course, is inadequate. There are many serious questions raised in the story that are not fully answered. Where did the serpent come from? Why is it that a serpent could speak to Eve? What was it about the fruit that did all the damage? These are questions that have been asked from the very beginning of the Judaic tradition.

One of the early attempts to answer them in Christianity was by Irenaeus in the second century. Irenaeus said that Adam and Eve were children originally and they were growing up. If they had gone on to reach maturity without falling, without disobeying God, they would have reached perfection. (This is exactly what the *Divine Principle* says, although Irenaeus understood it somewhat differently.) But a serpent came along and deceived Adam and

Eve into violating God's commandment, and they by their free will turned aside from God's commandment and as a consequence they died. God said, "On the day that you eat the fruit, you will die." Irenaeus said they died in two ways. First of all they died spiritually, and later they died physically.

Furthermore, they were afflicted with lust, because in the story of Genesis, immediately after eating the fruit, they covered their nakedness, indicating shame of their sexual parts. Irenaeus went on to explain that all the descendants of Adam and Eve were held in captivity by Satan until Christ came to liberate them. There are some problems with Irenaeus' story. First of all, it still doesn't explain where evil comes from. The serpent is already there, evil, and presumably created by God. Irenaeus frankly says the origin of evil is a mystery and we can't know the answer.

In answer to questions like, "Why are the descendants of Adam and Eve held in bondage?" his answer was that they all had sinned in Adam. This is the theory of seminal identity, but actually it creates more problems than it solves. Does it mean that all of us are pieces of Adam, or did Adam contain little seeds of every human being who is descended from him? How can you say that we sinned in Adam? These questions all remain in Christian theology.

Two centuries later Augustine tried to answer them. Using the same Genesis story, Augustine emphasized the free will aspect. The serpent is interpreted both by Irenaeus and Augustine as being Satan, the fallen angel, although it's a real serpent that Satan is using. For Augustine, Adam and Eve still died both spiritually and physically and their sin was transmitted to their descendants in one of two ways. Augustine never makes up his mind, he holds both a seminal identity theory and a theory of concupiscence. The very act of procreation is infected with sin because of concupiscence. Therefore all of the descendants acquire this sinfulness. But that has a problem too, because that means a physical act is contaminating man's spirit, which Augustine wouldn't grant.

One thing Augustine did was to really emphasize free will. In fact, Augustine emphasized it so much, that it turns out that the story in Genesis has nothing to do with the fall. Augustine said that Satan fell by his free will, but actually Adam and Eve decided to turn away from God before the temptation. The temptation actually had nothing to do with it. So when you follow Augustine's reasoning to its logical conclusion, it's just a question of spontaneous free will, and the story in Genesis is irrelevant.

Moreover, the doctrine of foreknowledge in Irenaeus and Augustine lead them to conclude that God *wanted* evil in the world, either as a justification for sending Christ, or to make the good appear more beautiful.

Another serious problem that both Irenaeus and Augustine have is that neither of them can explain why shame and concupiscence followed the fall. They come close when they say that because of their spiritual disobedience Adam and Eve incurred a physical disobedience: their flesh wouldn't obey their will. But logically, should that have manifested itself as gluttony if they had eaten a literal fruit? Why does eating a fruit lead to sexual lust? There's no connection there, and Irenaeus and Augustine were unable to make one.

The Unification view interprets the fruit symbolically, and says that God's prohibition was actually a command to Adam and Eve to refrain from a love relationship until they reached maturity. So, like the Irenaean view, Unification says that Adam and Eve were *growing* to perfection. God told them that if before they reached perfection they were to join together in a marital relationship — which was their ultimate destiny — they would short-circuit their love. Instead of joining themselves to God and then to each other, they would lose that connection with God. So according to Unification theology the serpent is a symbol for Satan, as in the other two versions. But in this instance Satan is Lucifer the archangel who actually developed a relationship with Eve. He was supposed to be Eve's servant, but he became envious of Adam and Eve because they enjoyed a special favor in God's eyes. The envy wasn't necessarily evil. For example, one could be envious of someone and want to emulate them or out-do them without necessarily having to destroy them. Envy can be used constructively or destructively. So Lucifer's envy, in the Unification view, was not evil at first. But his relationship with Eve gradually went past the point of God's prohibition, and Lucifer and Eve had something akin to a sexual relationship. At that point, Eve went to Adam, and induced Adam to have a love relationship with her. In a sense, Lucifer usurped the position of God in their relationship, and spiritually, the human race that descended from

Adam and Eve then had Lucifer in its lineage. As Jesus said, "You are of your father, the devil." Christ comes as a sinless man to become the new Adam, the source of the human race. There's more, but that gives you the main features of our understanding of the fall.

Darrol Bryant: Many questions come to mind, but I'm wondering if anyone wants to add a word about how that account of the fall links up with the practice of the Unification Church.

Jonathan Wells: In our practice, it means that the members of the Unification Church practice a very strict chastity. This is because we believe that our sexuality has to be restored. God originally intended for Adam and Eve to have a sexual relationship when they reached maturity. The fall was not sex itself but the prematurity of it. Restoration of that failure, then, requires a period of absolute chastity or celibacy to prepare ourselves for marriage by uniting with God first. When we reach sufficient individual maturity, then we marry.

Herbert Richardson: I'm a little confused about this pre-maturity thing. I'd like to know if Eve sinned because she had sexual relations before she was supposed to, or because she had sexual relations with a person with whom she was not supposed to. That is, let's suppose that Eve had become the right age. Then would it have been all right for her to have a sexual relationship with Satan? Because then it wouldn't be premature.

Jonathan Wells: No.

Herbert Richardson: Well, why not? You've stressed the prematurity factor, but it could go another way if we ask why did Satan seduce Eve sexually? Why didn't Satan just provoke Adam and Eve to have a sexual relationship with each other too early? I think that there's some kind of question here about whether it's the partner, or whether it's the prematurity.

Jonathan Wells: I think both elements enter into the picture. If we look at the probable dynamics of a boy and a girl growing to maturity, it's actually very unlikely that given God's command-ment they would have united prematurely without the presence of Lucifer.

Herbert Richardson: Yes, but the question is whether the presence of Lucifer couldn't have been just as efficacious in inducing them to have premature sexual relations with each other. One of the big problems in your account is how it is the case that there could be such a thing as a sexual relation between a flesh-and-blood woman and Lucifer who doesn't have a body? You then have to have some notion of spiritual sexual intercourse. You wouldn't have this problem, if you would go the route I suggested and have Lucifer *inducing* Adam and Eve to a premature sexual relationship.

Theologian X: You pointed out that both Augustine and Irenaeus seem to envisage the serpent as the real carnal form that Satan takes—I think one can construe Augustine and Irenaeus that way. I wonder if one of the reasons you might have referred to that was that in this version of the myth that you're offering it is thought to be the case that there was a carnal serpent who actually did, in some rather outlandish way, copulate with Eve? How do you deal with this formidable problem of envisaging a spiritual being having intercourse with a physical woman?

Jonathan Wells: I would have to argue that the idea of a sexual relationship between Eve and Lucifer is not all that implausible if we accept other biblical passages which talk about angels eating a meal, putting Jacob's thigh out of joint, and appearing in quite substantial forms to a variety of biblical figures.

Herbert Richardson: Can we have sexual relations today with angelic beings? Could you or I have a sexual relation with an angelic being today? Do we have any cases of it in the Unification Church? (laughter) I don't think it's just a funny thing, we really have a question. If you are really going to take this story in that kind of straight-forward, literal way and talk about it as the structure of reality, then it's a problem if those kinds of relationships have ceased.

Theologian X: I'd like to get back to hermeneutics again. Herb said that Jon was making a literal rendering of the text, but Jon himself said it was symbolic. I'd like to ask why the symbolism went in the direction it did when it could have gone in the other direction. For example, why are you concerned about the issue of sex at all? If we take Augustine and Irenaeus out of the picture for a minute and just look at the biblical text, there is no mention of sex at all. You interpreted the sense of shame, covering up genitalia with fig leaves, or whatever it was, as indicating that the original sin was sexual in nature. But certainly the text does not say that. If one is permitted a symbolic interpretation, which I think we have every right to—this shame, to me, most likely, is a shame for the broken relationship with God in its entirety, not sex in particular. First of all, phenomenologically, there's more than one reason that we might want to cover up our private parts. That is, it's not just for sexual reasons, but it also happens to be the dirtiest part of the body, too. And we know in some cultures, there are other reasons besides sex for covering up those parts of the body. But more important, in terms of interpreting the significance of the Adam and Eve story with the benefit of historical-critical analysis, is the insight that the Adam-Eve story is a microcosm of the history of Israel with God. Hence, the problem is the broken covenant. The commandment against adultery is only one small part of this very large and complex relationship with God. And the Adam and Eve story is a very simplified version of this. So it would be impossible to think of the sin of the human race over against God in its entire complexity being represented there in the story, and not simply premature sexual relations which I would see as only one aspect of sin.

Anthony Guerra: Could I speak first of all to the question of hermeneutics? The *Divine Principle* makes certain exegetical judgments in accord with some interpreters of the Old Testament that the words used in the Genesis account point to a sexual relationship as the origin of the human fall. Words like "to know," "picking the fruit" happen to be used in the original language to refer to a sexual relationship. Further, the history of religious analysis, the historical method, shows that there are exact parallels with other traditions in the area which are quite explicitly about a sexual relationship.

Theologian X: Yes, but the issue is idolatry. When Israel is in Canaan, the kind of religion that you have in Canaan is a fertility religion. The main dimension of the worship involved cultic prostitution. The first commandment has to do with which God you worship. So it's not fornication in the modern sense of violating a social moré, but it's fornication in the sense of actually choosing a religion other than the religion of Yahweh, and that's the reason for the profundity of sexual language there. It's not the same issue that we have today. The sexual language represents the entire confrontation of the religion of Yahweh with an alien culture.

Anthony Guerra: That's not my point. The point is what it meant then. Your interpretation is certainly plausible, but another interpretation is that it is a sexual relationship—and that it's referring to a concern for lineage, for families and a certain kind of adultery.

Virginia Hearn: I don't think Genesis 3 uses the verb "to know" in connection with Eve and Satan.

Mose Durst: I think the story can be interpreted in terms of the misdirection of love. Here's why. If the ideal of human growth is to perfect one's love, to manifest God's love and to become a reflection of that divine love, then the failure to reflect that divine love, the failure to mature, the misdirection of love, the idolatry of love focused on something other than divine love becomes manifest in the brokenness of one's will, the brokenness of one's relationship to the world. In Unification theology, the ground upon which we stand in relationship to the world is divine love. If we mature, then we can have a complete relationship to God, to each other and to the world, and understand our full value. If we misdirect that love, as happened in the Adam and Eve story in the temptation with the serpent, we don't reflect an eternal love, we don't reflect the universal love, we don't reflect the God-centered love but we reflect an idolatrous love. So it's both the partner and timing that's wrong. The direction, the attachment, the prematurity, all these things are misdirected.

Theologian X: Oh, I agree with that whole-heartedly, and I think you're right. My question was more formal. Why bother with all the fuss about the Adam and Eve story to say what you just said. I think what you just said is very fine, but I don't think we need these gymnastics with Genesis 3 in order to support that.

Mose Durst: Rev. Moon spent nine years in the hills of Korea meditating and praying about this. His great insight was that this in fact happened. For Rev. Moon the relationship of Lucifer and Eve was a real relationship, there was a real spiritual relationship between this being called Lucifer and the human being Eve and that central act took place. His revelation was understanding that it was a real act. We need to understand the significance of that real act in order not to do the same thing. By understanding the nature of the *specific* act rather than a general idea like pride, by knowing the specific act, we gain a certain power to withstand the temptation to repeat the act.

Darrol Bryant: What is the specific act that we might repeat? Would each of us repeat a relationship with Satan?

Mose Durst: Not necessarily with Satan, but premature love relations, the desire to enter into a love relationship that's immature

Neil Duddy: The main thing that strikes me as interesting, is that you have a device for exegeting that passage that leads to an "ideal." I believe that you pad the Scripture with other material. Thus when you read the Adam and Eve story you do so in terms of your most positive features: the ideal family and what it should be. So rather than focusing on what traditionally might be held as a negative aspect of evil, that passage has for you the purpose of providing a very positive vehicle for what life should have been like before the fall.

Herbert Richardson: I don't think that Unification theology actually derives from an interpretation of these texts Jonathan was using. I think that the texts on which it is based are different texts, texts which are usually completely overlooked in many Christian denominations.

The device is exactly what Dr. Durst was offering us. What is salvation? Look at Scripture and see what Scripture tells us salvation is. Salvation is portrayed in Scripture under the symbol of marriage. The eschatological banquet is a marriage banquet. We, in waiting for Christ, wait as the wise and foolish virgins. They are waiting for the coming of the bridegroom. The Song of Songs talks about the ultimate eschatological beatitude under the rubric of marriage. St. Paul talks about our being brides of Christ. In the Old Testament, the word for sin is adultery. The covenant is the bridal or the marriage covenant. The marriage imagery and symbols pervade the Scripture, and they are the ones that are finally decisive for describing what it is to be united with God. Then, at this point, you just make the obvious theological move and say, "Well, obviously, that which is most sinful is that which strikes most centrally at what salvation is." What is salvation? It is being brides of Christ. It is marriage with God. Therefore what sin is would be that which would most strike at the marriage union. What is that? Adultery.

In a sense, then, it isn't really read back in. One has to realize that the interpretation of a particular text in the Scripture doesn't rest just on what you find in that particular text, but rests on what you find in a number of other texts that are taken to illuminate it. It is the same as when you read a novel and try to understand a particular sentence. You don't understand the sentence by just taking it out and analyzing those words, you understand that sentence by understanding how that sentence functions in the story and relates to other things. Now, I think that in Christianity the teaching that salvation involves becoming united with Christ in marriage, with God in marriage, is at the heart of Scripture. I think that many churches have failed to emphasize this point. But they've only failed to emphasize that by failing to interpret certain kinds of texts in the Scripture. For example, who of us have heard preachers talk about the wise-and-foolish-virgins parable in terms of an eschatological interpretation? It's usually understood in a moralistic way. I think that's simply wrong, if you look at the Scripture. It is by a reading of the whole Scripture that one can rightly understand the text. Likewise, it is in the light of their whole reading of Scripture that Unification theology reads Genesis. That's where I think the matter rests.

However, there is another matter that hasn't come out here and that is that Unification theology is not so interested in the doctrine as in the behavior. What I'd like to ask at this point is this: if it is the case that salvation involves, not just marriage, but becoming brides of Christ, is it the case that in the Unification Church, the Blessing, the marriage ceremony is not just a union which puts two people together in marriage, but actually puts two people together in Christ? Is Rev. Moon functioning, in this way, as some kind of a Christ figure, so that when people are blessed, what is really happening is that they are getting united with Christ? It seems to me that if this is the symbolism of the Church, if it is, then it must be the case that the Blessing involves, not just people being united with each other, but also being united in some kind of mystical marriage with the one who represents the Christ. That's what I think is the case. Isn't that true?

Jonathan Wells: What do you mean by the one who represents the Christ?

Herbert Richardson: Well, I'm assuming that when Rev. Moon and Mrs. Moon perform these marriages that what is being created is the family. But it is very interesting what kind of family is being created. At the anthropological level, in an African tribe, when you get married to somebody, you don't just marry the person, you marry her whole family. Families get married. And it seems to me that within the Unification Church, the Blessing is not just understood as two people getting married, but they get married, in a sense, into the family, and I would think that they really marry Rev. Moon and Mrs. Moon. And the married couple, in a sense, become brother-in-law and sister-in-law to everybody else in the movement. It must operate that way.

Durwood Foster: You used another phrase that is intriguing to me, "in some mystical way." I think that begs a lot of questions, but it would be interesting to get some response on this from members of the Church.

By the way, let me say that I agree with your suggestion and your exposition that the doctrine of sin is really a reflex derivation from the vision of salvation. I think that's true at bottom in Unification theology as it's true in biblical theology. The story of the fall is there in Genesis 3 because in the dynamics of biblical theology it came in as a reflexive derivation from the vision of faithfulness to Yahweh. So there isn't a disjuncture between Unification and the Bible *hermeneutically* at that point. But to go ahead with my other point, what seems to be missing, if this is merely "some mystical way" in which the newly-weds are joined to the Rev. Moon, is the physical connection. Already with Christ, we did and do have a mystical connection, which many of us feel is sufficient, if I may say so. But what Unification theology seems to be proposing is that there is something drastically needed beyond that, namely a making good of what has gone physically wrong, the contamination that was originally introduced through the union between Eve and Satan. What would seem to be needed in addition to the mystical union with Rev. and Mrs. Moon, is some kind of physical union also. We might just leave that as a question. Is there any way in which the Unification interpretation seeks to supply that, or make good what otherwise seems to be a gap at that point?

Herbert Richardson: I'm sure we're moving into the area where everybody's getting very nervous. Everyone should realize why, when one comes down this road to see how the logic of this system works, people who've thought about this would suggest that there must be some sort of physical relation between Rev. Moon and Mrs. Moon and the other people. Then, they get involved in all kinds of fantasies which I think are mad, but I can understand why people get confused here. What is that physical relationship between Rev. Moon and the other people that must happen if the symbol system is genuinely to operate without a gap at this point?

Jonathan Wells: I think the best way I could describe it would be to use the traditional term, sanctification. But in the traditional Christian approach all we have is a spiritual union with Jesus. Wouldn't it be nice to have Jesus here with us, physically, in the room, directing us, kicking us, pushing us out to witness to Him, guiding our lives, inspiring us. The very fact that we're still fallen means that having a spiritual connection with Jesus while necessary, isn't sufficient. Our relationship with Rev. Moon is part of the sanctifying process, it's a very direct day-to-day transmission of a living tradition, a physical act of world-involving tradition. That's the relationship.

Neil Duddy: I think it's more than that though. The sacramental aspect in Christian life would illustrate a physical kind of relationship with Jesus. We eat His body and drink His blood, and some people think that it's really Jesus' blood. So that's moving along that path. I think there is some ceremony in the Blessing ceremony itself which does deal with that question. Now, whether we want to discuss that here, I don't know.

Herbert Richardson: I don't think that there's any need to talk about particular things, but just to know that there is something there, that the problem is recognized liturgically. I think what Jonathan said is absolutely right. The word is actually "attendance": to be in attendance upon and with this person in a living, loving way. I'm just struck by the wedding rings that are given by Rev. Moon both to the husband and to the wife, is that right?

David Kim: No, the rings are bought by Headquarters. They are not given to the bridal couple directly by Rev. Moon himself. People seem to make some kind of trouble or difficulty out of everything, and then put the blame on Rev. Moon. The real question is this: Why do we emphasize *all the time,* and *in every way* the fall of man? Because the fall of man is the very *cause* of the problem of this universe. God's heart is broken. His divine love toward mankind is lost. He is no longer sovereign. Satan is in the place of God, and the world has been in this mess for 6,000 years. It's really messed up! If you are a competent doctor, you have to diagnose the cause of the disease.

The Unification Principle gives some workable prescription for the cause of evil in the world. That's very important. In the family, husband and wife must be loyal and faithful to each other as life-time partners. If the husband goes to another man's wife every weekend for sex, or the wife changes her husband every week with another man for sex (this is actually happening in this adulterous world), then what kind of strange acts and behavior would result! This is just one example or illustration. What is the cause behind these real symptoms evident in our society? You have to know the cause in order to solve the problem. Like a criminal investigator in a criminal case, you have to find the causes, otherwise there is no real solution. Even though husband and wife may live together, and sleep together in the same bed, the problem still remains. So we must find the cause of these universal problems.

What do we teach in theology? What do courses in systematic theology teach in the seminaries? Fortunately or unfortunately, I have attended two seminaries since coming to this country in 1959 as a Unification Church missionary. I enjoyed systematic theology very much. Systematic theology teaches about Creation and the fall of man, about Jesus Christ and the Second Coming. The doctrine of the fall in systematic theology says that there is no solution to the fall of man, human theories cannot answer the mystery of the fall, only God knows. That was the conclusion then. The Unification Principle, however, explains and clarifies the true story of the fall of man. It is based not only on empirical data, but it is also biblically oriented. First of all: the fall of the first human ancestors actually took place. The story of the fall has to do with our ancestors' act of adultery or fornication. That is a revelation from God to Rev. Moon in his early years—a revelation from Jesus Christ and God. Many psychics or spiritually sensitive people in Korea and throughout the world, often saw in the past, and see even now, visions or scenes which took place at the time of the fall just as if they were watching a TV screen. These revelations and visions are seen and received by devoted Christian groups. They were revealed to one group of uneducated women during deep and intensive prayer, but these women were unable to interpret the scenes until they heard the adulterous act between Archangel, Eve and Adam explained by the teachers of the Unification Church.

Unfaithful acts between a husband and wife are adulterous and illegal even according to existing secular laws and constitute grounds for divorce and punishment. If someone takes another man's wife and commits adultery, he will break the law, isn't that so? The same thing applies to our first ancestors, Adam and Eve. According to the law of God, since the fall of man, Satan has been controlling mankind and the world for 6,000 years with his secret crime unexposed. Satan is using this as his weapon to control mankind. Sexual love is polluted by Satan. This most precious love now becomes the most dirty, and just as commercialized as the cheapest commodity. Recently in this country horrible pornography has been encouraging unnatural sexual relationships even between animals and human beings. Very recently one incident of pornography happened on one of the college campuses in New York City. Our CARP is fighting this issue now. In one of the on-campus student newspapers, a picture appeared in which a Catholic nun was masturbating with a crucifix, a cross. Nobody on the campus protested. They were afraid to speak out against such an insulting and blasphemous act. But Moon people got upset and involved themselves in the issue by making a big demonstration. We put up a fight. We aroused public opinion for the sake of Christianity and other religions. As a result of our initiative, that daily campus newspaper is suspended and is going to be out of publication soon. In other words, this kind of stuff is currently affecting whole campuses throughout the United States, not to mention in other countries.

Promiscuity and immorality are infiltrating everywhere. The Catholic faith was blasphemed and insulted, but no one from the religious world stood up and spoke out to confess and defend their own beliefs in the face of this kind of threat and challenge from Satan's power.

The fundamental problem of the universe begins with the fall of man. That is why we have to study the fall of man very thoroughly and diagnose it properly and precisely. Otherwise we cannot solve the problems. Where will the solution come from? Philosophy? It doesn't understand the fall of man. Sociology? It emphasizes phenomena and structure, and is not concerned with causes. Theology? It is the science of God, and I still believe in it personally. Of course I am conservatively oriented, but I believe a thorough study of human problems must come from the field of theology.

This is the reason why the Unification Principle emphasizes the fall and is very serious about it, and constantly talks about the fall of man as the root of human problems. The fall was a real incident. Because of the fall, Unification people believe, God is not liberated yet, and His creation is not complete. Satan is the god of this world, not God, our Heavenly Father. The Bible mentions clearly that Jesus is not the King of Kings, because the prince of the world is still Satan. Evangelicals must agree with us on this point. If we don't believe in the Bible, then we have no basis for discussion. If we believe in it, we must think seriously about the fall of man. Why do we emphasize this all the time? It is the root and the cause of the problem of the universe and mankind.

If we know what happened in the beginning, clarify the problem and solve it, God's love will directly come to us. The other Christians will be elevated to a higher level than where they are now. We Unification people are a little bit more advanced on this point. I prefer to call us Unification Christians. Unfortunately many Christians are persecuting us.

Theologian X: Just a moment! I thought it was a little more complicated than that. I just want to ask you this question. I agree that the fall is a problem. My only question is, why is the entire fall thought of in terms of only one sin, the sexual sin? Because there are all kinds of other sins that are in evidence.

David Kim: Adultery is the issue. Sex in itself is not *sin.* Sex at the wrong time, in the wrong place, with the wrong partner is sinful. This is the adultery, fornication and unnatural lust described in the Scripture. You have to go back to the purpose of God's creation, and find out why God created Adam and Eve, then you have to sort it all out and explain it logically and systematically. Our Unification message is, I believe, helpful in understanding the fall of man as the source of universal problems which surround mankind. We don't necessarily say that we have all the answers to all the problems.

Rev. Moon, although he receives many things from God, cannot say everything. Even Jesus said 2,000 years ago, "I have many things to say to you, but you cannot bear them..." Rev. Moon receives much knowledge from God, but he cannot tell all of it to his followers, just as in Jesus' time. In the book, *Divine Principle,* we have some of the things he received from God, and because of it, he is labeled the heretic of heretics, and is persecuted and accused as a seeker for political power, both by the traditional Christians and by the Fraser Committee.* Already with the *Divine Principle* book, we have too many problems with this world. Ten years ago the situation was much worse than at present, but still there are things in the *Divine Principle* book that are disagreeable to many people.

*Donald M. Fraser was Chairman of the Subcommittee on International Organization of the House of Representatives' Committee on International Relations when it investigated the Unification Church as part of an investigation of Korean-American relations.

Darrol Bryant: Several people want to respond. But please make it brief so we can take a break for coffee.

Anthony Guerra: Mr. Kim's contribution expresses one of the ways in which, if you read the *Divine Principle,* we approach the problem of sin. We look at the sociological phenomenon of the break-up of the family and we see this as a major factor in the decline of society. If you think about something which would be the most painful emotional experience in your life, then I think most people would say it would be if their spouse left them and had sexual relations with someone else. We might intellectualize about it, but people I know to whom that's happened have been torn up by it. I know a professor that's happened to, and it's one of the most painful things in his life. What the *Divine Principle* does in its doctrine of the fall is look at that psycho-social-spiritual phenomenon and say that's the symptom, what's the cause? Then, it goes back and says, here's the cause. That's, I think, the hermeneutic principle.

Theologian X: Why is the fall of man theologically equated with adultery when there are other sins to be accounted for?

Anthony Guerra: This is the point of keeping the story of the fall as a story. The way it's presented in the *Divine Principle* is as a kind of mytho-poetic expression, rather than a scientific, theological statement. It talks specifically about personal relationships. It involves both an ontology and specific human beings. If you read the *Divine Principle,* the problem of the fall is something which is a problem of the development of two human beings and their relationship with God and also with the angelic world. In this relationship there was supposed to be unity. They were the two beings who first had the spiritual capacity to relate to God as His children. They also, because they were the first, needed some kind of nurturing. Everyone else was going to have parents, how were they going to be raised up? How was God going to communicate to them? He was going to do this through the already created spiritual beings, i.e. the angels. So now you have the scenario: God who is the Creator-Father, the angelic world which is to assist in the completion of creation, that is, the perfection of Adam and Eve, and Adam and Eve who are to grow, reach perfection and marry. Now, the *Divine Principle* says that there began to be a problem in terms of the way the angel and Eve were relating, and also in the way Adam and Eve were relating. The *Divine Principle* says Lucifer became jealous of

Adam, there was envy. A whole number of sins that we normally talk about are put in the context of the disordering of personal spiritual relationships. The fall, or the premature sexual act, is simply the dramatic high point or consummation of that disordering, of that failure to center our lives in God. Why is it so critical? It is critical precisely because of what I spoke about before: the centrality of the family in the human order. Sin is what now perverts the unit that gives life to humanity: the family. Once that relationship is interfered with it has consequences. It is not a simple matter.

Theologian X: Let me just ask a quick yes or no question based on what Mr. Kim said. Do you permit or advocate interracial marriage?

Anthony Guerra: Oh, yes! Interracial marriage is central to what we are all about. What we are trying to do in marriage is to reconstitute the body of Christ, that is, the family of humanity as one family under God. At this latest matching* there were over 100 black people, and those black people were the first to be matched. Rev. Moon asked, "Who are the white people who would like to marry a black person?" Then many of them were matched interracially. Because we seek to constitute the body of Christ, the *one* family of humanity, of God, interracial marriage is seen as essential to that process of building a united humanity. In his speech at the Blessing, Rev. Moon spoke about the "love race." We must create a love race and a love culture: "What color are you? You are love color."

Patricia Zulkosky: At the same time there's no sense in which you are coerced to marry someone from other than your race, but it's perfectly open for you if you desire that.

Anthony Guerra: But it's really encouraged. This is one of the reasons I personally love Rev. Moon. There are a lot of liberal ministers I know, who get up and say, "We're for interracial unity," but I've never heard a minister say, "God would really like you white people to marry a black person." I've never heard any minister say that, except Rev. Moon.

David Kim: Actually Anthony's wife to be is Korean and he is Italian; Mike's wife to be is Japanese and he is American; Jonathan is engaged to an American woman. But all the matchings

---

*Reference is to the matching of 1410 members of the Unification Church by Rev. Moon on May 12, 1979, just three weeks prior to this conference.

are according to their wishes, no coercion is involved. I was with Rev. Moon for 15 hours during the matching process. I thought that my knowledge and skill in matching was 85% correct in the past, but this time I gave up and completely disqualified myself. I suggested quite a number of couples to Rev. Moon, but he had a far better idea, as I can now see from the fruits. I got only one out of 20 cases, and 19 cases I flunked. So Rev. Moon is the "heavenly matchmaker." I don't know why you got off in this direction from the topic of the fall of man. (laughter)

You theologians may like to know where Rev. Moon gets that kind of capability to make 705 excellent matches in 15 hours. I think you may be interested in what he said about it himself: "I have two special lenses..." Rev. Moon can see things spiritually and physically, and then match the candidates in all aspects of spirit and body. Right after the matching ceremony, during the State Directors' conference, he confessed, "I don't remember who is matched to whom anymore. I remember just one of the three famous Sheeran sisters, and she is working as a state director in West Virginia. The rest of them I don't remember." Here is my interpretation: When Rev. Moon stands up he acts as a channel for God in the matching process, the Spirit of God is working through him.

In some cases, people came back a second time for rematching after a disagreement between the two. "What happened to you?" Rev. Moon curiously asked one couple. The girl answered, "That brother rejected me." All during the long hours of the matching process, Rev. Moon remembered clearly whom he sent out with whom. Here is a very interesting and true story of which I was an eye-witness in Korea during the 1,800 couple matching. Once Rev. Moon recommended three matches, one right after the other. In their hurry and excitement, they somehow got mixed up on their way out of the hall, and couldn't remember which sister should go with which brother for consultation and talking. In a few minutes, wrong couples were formed before they went out of the hall. Suddenly Rev. Moon intervened in the mixed-up situation, and said as he regrouped the couples according to his original recommendations: "No, no, no, that one come here with this person, you go join that person over there..." In this way he cleared up all the confusion in the wrongly matched group. I was standing beside him, but didn't remember which one had been matched to whom. Rev. Moon remembered, though, precisely and in detail. I am totally amazed by his actions.

Therefore you have to remember that the matching process is not solely the doing of Rev. Moon himself, but is an act of God. God is alive and I believe God is using Rev. Moon because Rev. Moon's heart and love are directly connected to God. When he was 16 years old, still a young lad, he inherited a heavenly heart and heavenly secrets from Jesus and God. Unfortunately he is from the Orient, a yellow man, so many people persecute him in this country and throughout the world. If he were a white man, the Kingdom of God might already have been established! In conclusion, I personally believe that Rev. Moon's act in matching, engagement and marriage is truly an act of God. I have talked too much already.

Darrol Bryant: Let's break for coffee.

Hermeneutics and Eschatology

Darrol Bryant: We have an hour before we break for dinner. We are going to spend this time exploring Unification eschatology, their hermeneutics of the future. Since we are short on time, I'm going to ask Anthony Guerra to give us a thirty second outline of their eschatology. (laughter)

Anthony Guerra: How generous!

I think that probably the simplest way to explain our eschatology is to say that it's systematically related to the purpose of creation. That purpose is to establish the family of God, beginning with the original parents and then expanding out from those two original parents to a tribe, a nation, and finally a world. That world would be the world God originally intended. Our horizon in the present is focused on the original values which would have been realized in that original family, a God-centered family. The fall was explained as the dissolution of that original ideal of the family. Then, the process of reconstituting that original family is really the eschatological goal.

There's a notion again similar to what we find in Irenaeus — that in order to achieve restoration what must be done is precisely to reverse the problem that occurred in the original family. We've heard one part of the problem, which was the problem between Adam and Eve. But there is an additional problem which is central to our notion of restoration and that involves the Cain-Abel relationship. This is the problem of unity between the children. All humanity is symbolized by the children: Cain and Abel. The way Unification conceives of the restoration of that relationship is as follows: Abel made an offering to God which

God accepted, Cain's offering was rejected. God's original ideal was that Cain, rather than killing his brother, should have united in joy with his brother who had God's blessing upon him. Abel should have been humble before his brother and served him in such a way that he would have been able to empathize and be joyous with him in the blessing. If that had happened Cain and Abel would have united and experienced feelings of joyous brotherhood centered upon God. Now, that failed to happen. This model of Cain-Abel functions as the primary model for understanding the problem and for discerning the principles by which all conflicts can be resolved.

Unification theology argues that the ideal world is built around ideal relationships. That ideal world has both physical and spiritual dimensions. Religion, politics and economics are expressions of the spirit and the body and the relationships among men. All of these aspects of the world come under the Providence of God. The way God will now reconstitute the ideal is through the reversal of these failures, by reconstituting the original family, tribes and nations. Certain nations will serve as the Abel factor towards other nations who are in the Cain position. This principle of Cain and Abel is applied from individual relations to familial relations, to tribal, national and international relations. The goal is a just world. At the critical juncture, "the Last Days," there is a concentration of good and of evil, which may be the same thing as a concentration of power, such that the capacity of human beings for the realization of the ideal as well as for virtual destruction becomes available. That's the eschatological context in which former actions now take on a whole new dimension of significance. The only way to resolve this critical juncture is by applying the principles of unification. That, in brief, is my outline of Unification eschatology.

Darrol Bryant: What are some of the practical expressions of this notion of unification within the movement? I think you've suggested one thing already in terms of the promoting of inter-cultural marriages. Dr. Durst might want to say something about the things that are going on in the Bay Area family that are tokens of the movement towards a transformed world or building of the Kingdom. I think it might be helpful to know the sorts of things that you are doing which give concreteness to this larger theme.

Neil Duddy: It strikes me that the whole idea of the apocalypse, the Armageddon, has been by-passed. Could you say a little about that, which I know is a tenet that does appear in the *Divine Principle*.

Anthony Guerra: Yes, I think it goes this way. There is a notion that at the critical juncture in eschatological time there has to be this sort of Cain force, since all history has developed under this motif of Cain and Abel; there has to be a Cain ideology and world system, as well as an Abel ideology and world system, which can then relate to each other in the proper way of mutual service and love and accomplish the ideal world. One would represent a more materialist culture and a more atheistic-humanistic frame of reference. In this case we see that as communism. The other would represent a more spiritual theistic-humanistic perspective and value system and we see that as Christianity. Now, of course, we've had Cain and Abel factors throughout history. We've had atheistic-humanistic traditions and we've had theistic-humanistic traditions in, for example, the Renaissance and Reformation. The *Divine Principle* goes through a whole history of the development of atheistic and theistic ideologies as world systems, so what's special about our time? What seems special is that both have the conceptual and political capacity to embrace the entire world. In fact, there are two "world systems." That's what's crucial. At the same time, of course, we acknowledge the fragmentation in the communist block, and also a fragmentation within Christianity. Our view is not even conceived of in the same way that it was ten or fifteen years ago by Unification people. But we still operate with the same models.

Neil Duddy: In the *Divine Principle* it speaks about a Third World War in which there would be this opposition to communism and the final overthrow. Now I'm hearing a different interpretation. Are you saying that this is not necessarily going to come to pass?

Anthony Guerra: The *Divine Principle* has always said that it was an ideological war, not necessarily a physical war. What I'm suggesting is that in the present world situation, although we fundamentally use those categories, we acknowledge a kind of pluralism within communism that also needs to be accounted for. In fact, that is being accounted for by Unification thinkers.

Neil Duddy: Mr. Kim, do you see communism as the work of the devil?

David Kim: As Anthony just said a few minutes ago, the terms "devil," "Cain," "Abel" all have technical meanings in

Unification theology. The ultimate goal of Unification is to get rid of our Cain nature and to bring brothers into unity under God. That's the whole thing right there. So, Part II of the *Divine Principle* deals with the principles by which this goal is to be accomplished.

We understand ourselves as peaceful consummators of God's will. If everything is destroyed in the world, there will be nothing left for mankind. We say "love thy enemy," which is the teaching of Jesus, and we are going to practice it. We are very persevering people because we understand God's law of indemnity in human history. Even though our enemies are trying to destroy us with the backing of left wing and communist groups, we still pray for them just as Jesus prayed for his enemies because they didn't know God's will. Even on the cross, Jesus prayed for God's forgiveness for his enemies. So we Unification Christians are following his example.

Communists are the *war-mongers,* not us. We insist that we have to defend ourselves. When the free nations become sufficiently weak, the communists will try to conquer us since it is in the nature of communism. They will never change their tactics and their goal of conquering the whole world. Whenever their chance comes they want to conquer the whole world without God. But the ideology of Christ is to unite the world *centering on God.* The international dimension of both ideologies is similar, but the orientation is different. I don't say that communists are devils. Even good Christians, when evil influences them, become evil persons.

So then, what is evil and good in God's sovereignty? If anything adds to God's dispensation that becomes good; if anything is against God's will it becomes evil. This is the Unification definition. Jesus told Peter, "Get thee behind me, Satan." When Peter stood in opposition to Jesus and God's will, he suddenly became "satanic." Ideology comes first and is very important. World communism is based on an atheistic ideology and concept. According to God's will, the atheistic ideology must surrender to the theistic ideology.

We have to go back to the Garden of Eden and find the origin of sin. The fall of man induced the first murder between Cain and Abel. God must restore the damaged and lost relationships, otherwise He is not God. God is a God of principle and science. He preserves, controls and runs the whole universe based on the law. This teaching of the Principle of Restoration through Indemnity (Part II of the *Divine Principle*) contains very profound and deep points of the *Divine Principle*. Rev. Moon explored it and found out answers to fundamental questions about the universe and man, and finally God approved it officially. This is the spiritual law that still applies up to the present.

Rev. Moon said in his public speeches that he came to America as a fire-fighter because this nation is in danger and the American people are completely ignorant of the nature of communism and of the threat to America. America must have ideological supremacy over the atheistic side. Thus the original Cain and Abel relationships in God's dispensational course must be restored. But the Cain side representing evil will never just give up, they will continue their aggression until they no longer see any hope for victory. In other words, if the supremacy of free nations over communist nations is not maintained, they will risk war. Therefore our church is giving a strong warning. We must have supremacy in both ideology and military strength over communist nations. In this way we will prevent a war which would be disastrous for all mankind. This is the Unification position on the possibility of war.

In the meantime, we have to try hard to maintain peace and freedom in the world. We believe in democracy which is based on Christian concepts: human rights, individual freedom of worship and religion. Communism, on the other hand has the clear goal of world conquest centering on a God-denying ideology. It's now one of the most powerful dynamics in the world. Even the largest democratic nation, America, did not defeat a small communist nation in the recent war in Vietnam. If there had been a more active and genuine Christian movement against communism, its successful expansion on the international level could have been prevented. We are worrying about this point.

Our bitter and sorrowful experience during the Korean War taught us what communism actually is. We don't care as much about the doctrines and theories of Marxism and Leninism, as we are deeply concerned about their evil practices. Therefore all Christians should have one central motto: "We must overcome the evil of communism." Unification people believe that we can convert even the communists to the Christian ideology. The reasoning of communists is wrong. They deny God. A simple illustration can make this point a bit more clear. You and I have a real physical father who is alive, but suppose someone were to say, "You have no father." We just cannot accept that argument.

Rev. Moon says that the reason for world communist expansion derives from the failure of modern Christianity. Christian churches are challenged by reform movements, by new interpretations of the Bible and new religious movements as part of God's dispensation to the degree that modern Christianity failed in its heavenly mission.

I hope this answers your questions even if it is a rather long remark. Anyway, we Unification people are peacemakers. We don't want Christians to be killed by communists, as has happened in the past and is happening in contemporary times.

Darrol Bryant: I think that your anti-communism is one of the more controversial aspects of this movement. Another controversial aspect of the movement is its apparent concern to create business and economic institutions. What, many ask, does this have to do with the coming of the Kingdom of God? Would someone care to speak about this? How does having a cleaning company, as I understand you have in the Bay Area, build the Kingdom of God?

Jonathan Wells: I think theologically the root of the question is in the real success story of the Bible: the story of Jacob and Esau. Here you have two brothers united by the power of love. They were separated just like Cain and Abel, just like the Archangel and Adam. This same pattern runs through the Bible. Jacob, being the younger of the two, was chosen and was able to win the blessing. That restores the lineage. The first-born represents the first fallen act of Satan or Lucifer, the second-born represents God's side. So what does Jacob do? He works for twenty-one years to win the material blessing. He gains a family and material things. Then he comes back from exile and his brother still wants to kill him. His brother is materialistic. He's the guy who sold his birthright for a pot of lentils, he has that kind of nature. Jacob, in his wisdom, understanding God's principle, realizes that the only way to win his brother's heart is through material things. He sends over first some of his servants and flocks, as if to say, "Here, I love you." His brother accepts them, but is still uptight. Then he sends over more of his possessions, and Esau begins to think, "Hey, this is not bad!" Finally Jacob sends over his family. They say, "We love you. These are gifts from your brother." Esau, who has been standing there with 400 armed men ready to pounce on Jacob, capitulates. Jacob is able to win his brother's heart and restores that relationship. That becomes the victory of God.

This sets a pattern for restoration. This is behind the Unification effort to restore a material foundation, like business, and establish an economic foundation. In order to overcome a materialistic ideology in this country and elsewhere, we've got to be able to express Christian love in real ways. That's what Marxism is doing in South America and Africa: winning people by materialistic means. If we recognize that we are, in a sense, in that Abel position, that we are like the Jacob of today, and communism represents the position of Esau, somehow we have to be able to restore that relationship. Material things are then, from this perspective, important. Furthermore, America's wealth is a blessing from God. America's blessing is a material blessing for the world. For God to be able to continue to bless this nation, America should use her blessing well for God's purposes. That's theologically important.

Durwood Foster: Just a couple of comments. First: there is a very widespread and growing consciousness today in the world of the necessity of uniting the spiritual and material. One should celebrate the way in which the Unification movement is expressing that and contributing to that. Richard Quebedeaux was talking last night about the young Evangelicals; this is what they are trying to do. Liberation theology is doing this. Sri Aurobindo in India, and Neo-Hinduism in general, is attempting to integrate the ideal and the real. There is a world-wide movement of consciousness in this direction. It's right that the Unification movement also is promoting this and attempting to provide a theoretical-theological base for it. I think that the theoretical-theological base that can do the most justice to this issue will be the one that ultimately emerges as the appealing one and the helpful one for the world as a whole. One question I wanted to ask was whether in the Unification eschatology it is envisaged that the realm of God will be established within time and space; that is, whether this realm is looked forward to as a utopia that can and will actually be achieved under historical conditions? The theology that I mainly studied in my own seminary days denied that and critiqued that kind of utopianism very sharply. But there's been a kind of reaction against that today within Christian churches also.

Mose Durst: One of the great appeals of the Unification Church to me, from my Jewish background, was the messianic ideal for the world, not a fixed point at which things stopped, but rather a point of maturity at which time things began. In a mature culture, growth and development are continuous. The quality of culture will continue to improve based on a certain foundation. The ideal of our life is that knowledge is good, and its purpose is to teach us how to love. Therefore, all professions are helping professions, and all activities are ideal, loving activities, which follow from God's heart. If knowledge is centered upon love, a standard of divine love brings the supreme value. A theory of art, for example, is centered not only on aesthetics, but also involves ethics. By having the aesthetic dimension centered upon an ethical value structure, art becomes the new art for the new age. Our projects in the Bay Area, like Project Volunteer, have the motto: "public service with commitment of heart." Education is not only technical education, it's ethical and heartistic education. In every dimension, in every area, we seek to work in the world to transform culture. If the media is not operating to its full potential, we have to develop a daily newspaper in New York City to help promote a new standard of value for what media can be. If art is not functioning well, we have to have a Manhattan Opera Center, with an inspired operatic artist like Ron Paquette. If churches are not functioning to their full potential, then we have to start the Holy Spirit Association for the Unification of World Christianity, unifying race and culture. All of these issues need to be addressed. The International Cultural Foundation seeks to bring sciences together. Conferences like "The Unity of the Sciences and the Search for Absolute Values" seek to direct sciences once again to value questions. In all of these dimensions we see the necessity of transformation. We've got to take culture as it is and move it up to a new level. We have to take responsibility for our individual consciousness. I've started a Creative Community Project here as an attempt to take my training in humanistic psychology and apply it to a new vision, a deeper vision. Rev. Moon doesn't call us in the morning and say, "Look, you get out there and do this." I'm inspired by an ideal and I have the responsibility of translating that ideal into economics, politics, culture. When I go into my office before teaching I close the door and pray to be inspired to serve my students more.

Durwood Foster: I want to make it clear that I approve of all of these things and celebrate them, but I'm asking at the moment whether Unification is a new utopianism. This may not seem a very important question to many people, but it's a question that theologians get curious about occasionally. It seems to me that in many respects Unificationism is a utopianism. That is to say, you are working towards an actual state of affairs in history and society that you think can be achieved and will be achieved. And at one time you were very sanguine about how soon it might be achieved. I don't know if there has been some sobering up of this mood more recently or not, but that's beside the point. It's this question of utopianism specifically that I was wondering about.

Anthony Guerra: The problem with the idea of progress in history is that one feels that it doesn't take account of sin, of the potency of sin. There has been a long-standing general critique of certain notions of progress that I think has a lot of validity. Now Unification does hold that the Kingdom will be established within the historical order. At the same time, we have a very respectful view of the power of sin. The establishment of the Kingdom can only take place with an internal resolution of the problem which is simply what we've been talking about in terms of the fall, and then the establishment of families. We see that as a resolution of the deep-rooted problem of disoriented love. Furthermore, there's a heavy emphasis on the need to sacrifice, which is usually lacking in the Enlightenment notion of progress. Even the model that was talked about — Jacob/Esau or Cain/Abel — says that the way to overcome the deep-rooted sinfulness — which I interpret to mean the kind of non-loving, hateful relationships that exist between races and between third-world nations and wealthy nations—is through a great price of sacrifice on the part of the wealthy nations, or the white race. It's going to demand sincere and deliberate sacrifice. The theological notion is that God is not just concerned with the direction of individual lives, which traditional Christianity has emphasized, but He's also concerned with the direction of tribes and nations. Through that providential direction that kind of utopia (if you will, though I think "utopia" is a bad word because it means nowhere and we're talking precisely about it happening here) can be achieved. But that can only happen through this larger providential direction. I think the real question is therefore, "How does one know about God's providence?" We have to answer this in order to be connected to it. Also, how do nations learn about it?

Mike Mickler: I think that within Unification theology, despite the clarity of the models and the understanding of God's providence, there is still space for surprise in terms of the Kingdom coming. In reading some of the liberation theologians, I was interested to see the use that they make of the word "utopia". For them, utopia seems to be something that undermines the established order, and not necessarily something that is going to be established by human means.

I think we do articulate a utopian vision in somewhat that fashion: to undermine structures that are simply exploitative and unjust. I know that Rev. Moon is always willing to sacrifice the Unification Church. I don't see how a group of just several thousand full-time members or however many members there are in the United States can physically usher in the Kingdom in our lifetime. But we can lay a certain foundation that we can build on. I do think that through the articulation of our utopian vision we have already shaken a lot of the established structures of this country in a lot of different ways and we continue to do that.

Herbert Richardson: You haven't mentioned what seems to be the most radical element in the Unification vision of restoration. Who's against anything you've said? But the thing that Unification theology says that is so surprising and that will shock everybody is that you even believe that you can redeem the past and the dead. It is probably the case that the first emphasis within the Unification vision of restoring the world is the restoration of the dignity of the life and work of those who went before us. How is that accomplished? This task is accomplished by taking up their task and completing it, thereby redeeming them and fulfilling them. There are all kinds of discussions about how one redeems ancestors, but I just would make the point that probably the best way to understand what Rev. Moon is doing is that Rev. Moon has taken up the task of redeeming the work of Jesus Christ. Jesus came to do something—He clearly wanted to do more than He was able to do — He did all He could in the time that He had, and He was waiting for someone who would take up His vision and work in order to bring all that He had done to true and ultimate fulfillment. One of the great sources of power within the Unification movement is that, after all, there are all these ancestors rooting for us. We also have some, unfortunately, who are rooting against us, but they are our people, too. But we have all of these ancestors, who inspire us and who fill us with the will to carry forth the work. So, for example, we're not a few thousand people. We are a few thousand people here now with millions of people there working to support us. Now, of course, that's the Christian doctrine of the communion of the saints, to some extent. It's also the Oriental doctrine of respect for ancestors and their labors. And I think it's also a kind of Jungian insight into the influence of our past and the elements within the collective unconscious and the whole cultural past that we are concerned with. I think that one gains a gigantic power within a movement when it feels connected this way with the past.

I remember an essay by Metz, (the Catholic Marxist theologian) who in that essay in *Religion and Political Society,** asks who in the midst of all the talk about liberation is finally going to have the courage to talk about the liberation of the dead? Well, let's talk about it. What is the liberation of the dead? It's taking up that for which they gave their life and making it your responsibility so that their vision in life might find fulfillment. I think that should be talked about. It's a very much needed message in America. This is where some of the misinterpretation of the Unification Church comes in. In talking about the past in Unification theology it's not only talking about the past, but also about our responsibility for the future. That's what renders it different from either a conservative group, which talks about the past for the sake of the past, sacrificing the future, or a liberal group, which talks about the future for the sake of the future, sacrificing the past. It's a group that really has a sense of life in time.

Virginia Hearn: I would like to ask if this is the heart of the Christian Gospel. If we have this goal of a beautiful world, is it imminent if enough of us join together and make some sincere, deliberate sacrifice for it? Is this the Gospel?

Jonathan Wells: I think that what you describe is necessary but not sufficient. This leads into the whole question of the second coming of Jesus, and what role that plays in God's providence. We're talking about setting up the Kingdom of Heaven on earth and the fulfillment of human history in the Last Days, and yet it seems that the traditional Christian message is that only Jesus does this, that Jesus Himself comes again to do this.

Religion and Political Society, Jürgen Moltmann, et. al., New York, N.Y.: Harper & Row, 1974.

Theologian X: When you say that Jesus comes again how do you mean that? Is it not your interpretation that, as far as the Second Advent is concerned, this office would be held by Rev. Moon who would be acted upon by Jesus, is that the interpretation? Or is Rev. Moon considered as Jesus? You are not saying that, are you?

Jonathan Wells: No, Rev. Moon is not considered to be Jesus. Your first description is probably a good way to put it, that is, he fulfills an office. The office of the messiah is understood more in an Old Testament sense. Now we are back to our hermeneutical problem. The thrust of the New Testament witness seems to be that this same Jesus will return. But what happened at the *first* coming? Two thousand years ago people were waiting for the messiah quite consciously. They knew Elijah would precede the messiah because Malachi had said so. In fact, there's nothing in the Old Testament to indicate that anybody but Elijah would precede the messiah. So when Jesus came, he had to tell people that in fact John the Baptist was Elijah, and he does this in Matthew. So actually a different person fulfills the role that was dictated by the Old Testament prophecy. The *Divine Principle* interpretation of passages in the New Testament about the Second Coming of Jesus makes a parallel between His times and our times comparable to the relationship between Old Testament prophecy and New Testament prophecy. Though we believe that the coming of Jesus was the coming of the Messiah, we believe that the person who comes to fulfill the Second Coming may well be different from the historical Jesus of Nazareth.

Herbert Richardson: Now, I think that's wrong myself. You've probably even heard me lecture this at Barrytown. I think that the coming again of Christ is not the coming again of another person fulfilling the office of the Christ, namely, Sun Myung Moon coming to fulfill the Christ office. Rather I think the teaching of the *Divine Principle* is, though not worked out specifically because it is not worked out in relation to the set of questions under the doctrine of the communion of the saints, that the person of Jesus has sought out and united Himself with the person of Sun Myung Moon, such that, using Pauline language, there is an indwelling of Jesus in Sun Myung Moon and an indwelling of Sun Myung Moon in Jesus. Hence, Moon might say, as Paul said, "I, not yet I, but Christ in me. I yet not I, but Jesus in me." I believe that the union between Jesus and Sun

Myung Moon, by virtue of the indwelling of the two, leads to something like a double personal identity. "I, yet not I, but Jesus in me." I think that what Sun Myung Moon does, is done, not by Sun Myung Moon, but by Jesus in him, or by Sun Myung Moon and Jesus in him. This is not a strange way to talk because every Christian everywhere talks in this way. "Well, it's not my work, but the work of Jesus within me." I think that Jesus is working in everybody this way, and that the coming again of the messiah may quite reasonably be interpreted within Christian orthodoxy, not as His coming again in a separate flesh, but as His coming again in the spirit to indwell us in a real personal way such that we live, yet not we, but Jesus in us. It's true that I believe that Jesus is working in Sun Myung Moon, trying to fulfill His purposes and might conceivably do it.

Can I tell a story of yours, Darrol? Darrol told me this story, it's a marvelous story. He said he was asking a young member of the Unification Church about Sun Myung Moon, and who she thought Sun Myung Moon was, and how she got this straight with the Second Coming. This student said, "I believe they are the same." This is a very simple 18-year-old girl. And you have to apply a kind of hermeneutic. Obviously she knows that Sun Myung Moon is not Jesus. We've got pictures of Jesus and Moon and they look different. (laughter) What is she saying? She's saying something that's the expression of a profound spiritual insight, namely, that it is true in our life that Christians from the past returned and so entered into the lives of others, that we say, "Yes, that's Jesus." I think that's the orthodox doctrine of the communion of the saints, and I think it's a perfectly reasonable explanation. I don't understand why there would be any trouble with it at all.

Mark Juergensmeier: But there remains a fundamental issue. I know theology is the art of the ambiguous, but essentially the issue is about the nature of revelation, whether it's special or whether it's universal. Every tradition has to grapple with that in one way or another. One way of obscuring the problem is to couch the nature of revelation in such a way that leaves room for ambiguity. But within the ambiguity, the conflict remains. Either revelation is located in time and space within a person, or it is located in a more generalized kind of way, within epochs or within a quality of the condition of the self. You either have it one way or the other. You hold traditions together precisely through the ambiguity, but I think individuals take their stand, and I think that student thought that Moon was Jesus, that the revelation occurred in a specific location in time and space. I assume that your interpretation is more universal, that the Holy Spirit works in a more generalized kind of way and may occur in many persons at one time. That's one difference, and it will always remain despite theologians.

Herbert Richardson: I think it's a very reasonable difference. But I don't think it's one way or the other, I think it's a matter of more or less. How can I say that? The teaching of the New Testament is that every Christian is one who, at least in principle, is indwelled by Christ and indwells Christ. Not only that, but all of the saints come to indwell us. There's a degree of more or less in the lives of people depending on their spiritual maturity.

Mark Juergensmeier: That tradition holds a contradiction. I'm not faulting Unification for developing this tradition. But I think it does what every tradition does, and has to do: that is, put together within language what essentially are contradictory elements. That's part of the delight of theology or our faith. If it were not contradictory, if there were not intentions of paradox, there would not be much fun to it. You'd take it or you wouldn't take it. There would be nothing to explore, it would be all terribly obvious.

Darrol Bryant: I'd like to finish the story and relate it back to Virginia's original question of what constitutes the Good News. Is this the Christian Gospel that we're talking about in talking this way? It seems to me that within the context of Unification theology, there are some very obvious things to say. The first is simply, "Yes, this is the Christian Gospel," Why? Because the Unification Church, or at least the way I read the *Divine Principle,* maintains that it is Jesus who restores man to God. That's one of the things that this Christian group would share with all other Christian groups and it is very central to the notion of the Gospel. What do we take, in terms of the New Testament account of Jesus as central to Jesus' life and mission? Well, as I was talking to this girl, I asked her this because she was a young girl who had come from a rural area north of Toronto. I was curious as to how she was putting together her Baptist background and her membership in the Unification Church. I asked her what the difference was between Rev. Moon and Jesus, and she said she thought they were the same person. As we talked more, it came out that who and what Jesus was, was that He's a great teacher of love. That was her understanding of it.

Mark Juergensmeier: It doesn't make any difference what her understanding of it was. For example, if I were to say that I see Christ in Christians, that's all very well for me, but that doesn't make me a Hindu. In other words, it seems to me that a tradition defines itself from within its tradition. What would make me a Hindu would be whether or not the tradition of Hinduism could understand my acceptance of seeing Christ in Christians as a part of their revealed authority, if you could use that term, or in line with the basis of authority within the Hindu tradition. I think that's always the way in which Christianity as a tradition understood what is or is not in the tradition.

Darrol Bryant: I don't see the analogy. You're talking about two distinct religious traditions and how one recognizes, acknowledges, or accepts the other on the basis of their authorities. I don't start with that premise when we're talking about the Unification Church. It's not like Hinduism or Buddhism that we have to try to get related to the Christian tradition. The Unification Church emerged in the context of the Christian traditions of Korea. Now the question is what we in other Christian traditions do with what they are saying.

Mark Juergensmeier: The issue of a new revelation becomes very important here. If one sees the revelation within the Unification tradition as an extension of and essentially based on, or in some sense a re-creation of the original revelation of the biblical tradition, then what you say would be the case. If you see it as extra revelation, that is, as a revelation like that of the Latter Day Saints, then you get into precisely the kind of tension that the Mormons do: whether they are Christian or not Christian.

Durwood Foster: I think Mark would have been very interested in the discussion this morning because we did focus on the problem of revelation and authority at that time. This is still relevant because you never get to a point where it's not relevant. However, now I want to comment on the specific matter that Herb was talking about with respect to the indwelling of Jesus in the believer, or in personal life today.

I think Christian theological language is in some respects extremely untidy on these points. That's not surprising because of its immensely variegated historical development, with many cultural streams coming into it, reaching over two millennia. It seems to me that the situation basically with respect to the return of Jesus is that there are two lines of thematization that deal with different problems. Herb has, in fact, coalesced these. In some ways it's useful to do that, but in some ways it obscures the difference to which the two lines of thematization initially and continually were trying to address themselves. One way in which phraseology about the return of Jesus has functioned has been parallel to the way in which the phraseology about the Holy Spirit has functioned. That is, it was the Christian experience that after the events named death and resurrection, there was an experience of Christian participation in the reality that had been present in Jesus as the Christ, and that was variously called "the dwelling of Jesus Christ in you," "the indwelling of Jesus," "the indwelling of the Holy Spirit." There are several variations in Christian phraseology that express that kind of experience, which is terribly important to the Christian life. But on the other hand, there's another line of thematization that has to do with the wrap-up of the historical process, the final fulfillment of God's purpose in creation and in history. It so happens that the same language got used to deal with this problem, the return of Christ at the end of the Age to judge the quick and the dead, and so on. There has been in modern Christian theology an attempt to coalesce these two lines of thematization. C.H. Dodd, for example, undertook this with his view of realized eschatology. But I think the view of Christian history on the whole, and the judgment of modern scholarship, is that you can't totally collapse these two lines of thought into each other. In addition to the indwelling of Jesus in the believer — something that was experienced from very soon after the crucifixion up until now — there's also some point in raising the question and talking about the way in which history is finally resolved or wrapped up or ended in the sense of being fulfilled. It is this second sense in which the doctrine of the return of Christ at the end of the Age has functioned. By going at it the way Herb has you're kind of leaving that whole problematic out of the picture.

It seems to me that in the beginning of the Unification movement it was this second thing that was being talked about. Dr. Young Oon Kim also spoke of this very emphatically the time I was in Barrytown, so that to me that is still a problem. It is not totally covered by the very true things that you, Herb, have eloquently said. There's still this other usage and problematic focus that needs to be dealt with.

Herbert Richardson: I would think that the doctrine of the Second Coming is not, in the New Testament, tied up with the end of historical time, but it is tied up with, as you said yourself, the end of the Age and the introduction of a New Age of history. Now, it seems to me that it's only when you forget the idea of the millennium that you get this problem with the realistic-futuristic language. It was later Christian theology that tied this language up in a speculative way with history, that Jesus is going to come back at the end of *all* time. It seems to me that in Scripture that language that is futuristic in that way is not tied up with the end of history, but it's tied up with the end of a particular cultural epoch which is going to be succeeded by another cultural epoch called the millennium. Though I think that the question of what is going to happen at the end of time is a very real question, it seems to me that it is not biblical to use the Second Coming imagery at that point.

Durwood Foster: Your point is well taken. It would force the concession — I mean, it doesn't have to be forced, it would be gladly made — that there are various species of the second kind of thematization that I was talking about. The one in which the end of the Age would be understood as the absolute cessation of historical time would be only, at best, one of the species. But I was only attempting to differentiate that whole bracket of thematization from the other one into which I thought you had collapsed it, namely the indwelling of Jesus in the heart of the believer.

Theologian X: I wouldn't concede that much because the apocalyptic horizon stands behind so much of that language in the New Testament and that's more than the end of a cultural age! That vision involves an ontological change when the lion lies down with the lamb, when tears are wiped away forever and ever, and health is distilled in the dew. All of these images are there. There's more than just a shift from one epoch to another being supposed in Mark 13, Matthew 24-25.

Herbert Richardson: I don't agree with you at all. I think that that's the shift from the epoch before the millennium to the epoch of the millennium, not the shift from the historical age to the post-historical age, the shift from time to eternity.

Jonathan Wells: My point is that this debate is quite important, and also very Christian. Another question that raises itself here, and I think this was Mark's concern, is, can the Unification proposal in this debate be a part of the Christian debate, or is it a totally different ball game? Every time I begin discussing eschatology with a heterodox group of Christians I find that the heterodoxy becomes aggravated by the subject. There's a tendency, I find, for people to hear the Unification proposal and automatically reject it as non-Christian, when actually if they heard each other's proposals, they would probably denounce them as non-Christian too.

Darrol Bryant: They have, in fact, done that.

Theologian X: One of the interesting things I've seen with my three-hour old understanding of the *Divine Principle* is that there's a dual track in Unification thinking regarding the Kingdom. As I understand the Principle, the tragedy or the triumph of Jesus was an option portrayed in the prophecy of the Old Testament. People could have accepted Him as their king with a triumphal entry into Jerusalem straight from the beginning. Or they could take the other option, the tragic option, that He would be on the cross. These are the two bifurcated options that Jesus had, as prophesied in the Old Testament. If that's the case, I would suspect that the same thing holds true for the eschatology of the Unification Church, and that's why there's the enigma in the title, "Lord of the Second Advent." It could go either way. It's almost like a self-disclosure of Jesus again. And if that's really the case, then the advent of the Kingdom through the Unification Church is also subject to the same type of tragedy. Thus we're on wheel 84 of new attempts: you know, second lord of the advent, third lord of the advent, fifth lord of the advent, and so on down the line. I think that creates an enormous problem in appreciating where the Kingdom is really coming from.

Dagfinn Aslid: I would like to make a little more explicit some elements of our eschatology. One thing that I think you clearly noticed is the use of typology as a heuristic tool. "Cain-Abel" is a device which I suspect for most Christians today is dead, but it is alive and well in our theologizing and in our history. I think this is very characteristic of our movement. Our use of these constructs as heuristic tools could, and I think should, be critically discussed. I find them very fruitful, but there is also danger when you start speculating about nations, "archangel nations and Eve nations," "Cain and Abel" nations. There are these two sides. On the whole, however, I think it's a fruitful thing. Connected with that, I'd like to make an observation concerning the mode of theologizing that I've often noticed in Rev. Moon. It is one of playfulness. There's a very lush and free imagination at work and often very surprising concepts emerge from that playfulness. Oftentimes he would come up to Barrytown and sit down under the trees, and would speak. Often he would play with theories about the length and curvature of noses and himself as an enigmatic somewhat mysterious person. And I think that was instructive to many of us. There's a danger of becoming overly serious about something that is, in a sense, very playful. I think that's one aspect of the way we go about theologizing that people often miss. We like to play around with these tools and sometimes what comes out makes a lot of sense, sometimes it doesn't. Therefore, I tend to be reserved on the question of whether or not the Unification Principle is a new truth or a perennial philosophy. I think it's a start. Since I have some background in music, I tend to look at it as a sensitivity. I liken it to Dixieland jazz where you have what we musicians call progression. I see the revelation as like a core progression upon which we improvise. There are a lot of new possibilities and that's one of the very inspiring things to me about a group like this. When we meet with traditional theologies we see the fruitfulness of these concepts. They tend to come alive, and you can see their usefulness. It's sometimes hard to keep silent because I find that the *Divine Principle* provides us with such exciting tools. It tends to generate ideas and concepts where before one would just hear a concept and say, "ho hum." There wouldn't be that kind of heuristic and hermeneutic encounter, nor would we see a new understanding coming alive. Finally, I would like to just briefly mention the radical importance given to human beings in our eschatology in relation to the fulfillment of the eschaton. Ours is not an apocalyptic vision. We don't believe that the Kingdom arrives through a supernatural intervention. That results in a realization of some utopia independent of what we do about it. I think we ought to underline the radical importance of our response and sensitivity to the eschatological *process!* It is more a process than an event. Consequently, if our responses are not there, things just don't work right. This notion is very important. It necessitates an attitude which isn't content with contemplation, but seeks to be very active to realize this purpose of God. Unless we put these principles into reality, they aren't really true. Rev. Moon has mentioned this, too, quite often. What we are dealing with here is not speculative knowledge, it is knowledge that is responded to, and only true to the extent that it is lived.

Darrol Bryant: We are just going to have to stop here.

Witnessing, Evangelizing and Formation:
The Hermeneutics of Style

Darrol Bryant: The first thing that I want to do is thank you, Dr. Durst, for this marvelous meal. I thought we might shift our focus somewhat this evening to the question of the lifestyle of the Unification movement. One of the ways to understand a movement other than looking at its theology is to look at its practice. We might call this the "hermeneutics of style." Anyway, I thought we might direct some specific questions to Dr. Durst about the Unification movement in the Bay Area. This seems to be the most controversial center, the most controversial part of the Unification movement in the United States. Let me begin by asking you, Dr. Durst, to say something about the kinds of institutions and organizations and communities that are a part of the movement here. Then, secondly, would you say something about the charges that have been leveled against the Creative Community Project? In particular, the charge that it is being deceptive because of its failure to make explicit its connections to the Unification Church.

Mose Durst: One of the things that inspired me about the Unification Church is that it was a movement to transform culture. When I saw things like the International Conferences on the Unity of the Sciences, the International Cultural Foundation, opera centers, Freedom Leadership Foundation and the *News World,** I saw the attempt to take every dimension of culture and

---

* *The News World* is a New York City daily newspaper that began publishing Dec. 31. 1976. It is connected with the Unification movement.

to transform it. It was belief, from my own Jewish background, that religion if it was to have any meaning at all, had to have meaning in every dimension of life. The orthodox Jews perform 613 blessings. No matter what you do—wake up in the morning, read the newspaper, start your tape recorder — you say a blessing, every dimension of life has a sense of holiness. I was frustrated in art and teaching in that I could not experience that wholistic sense of life. I had training in humanistic psychology. I had been involved with many things. When I came into the Church, I felt that the principles of the movement were applicable to politics and economics. One could view the Principle as a management principle. I've had some training in management theory and I direct a small non-profit management corporation. The Principle is a management principle. It's management by objectives in the best sense. I always felt the necessity to deal not only with the Church as a church but also to relate the Church to many other areas of life.

I began with Dr. Bergman and some other people, "Judaism in Service to the World," which is my attempt to bridge the Jewish-Christian argument. That corporation is a non-profit corporation and still exists. I naively never realized how much hostility it would bring from the Jewish community. So very quickly, after I had seen the hostility, I down-played it. In fact we had a concert in which we brought the Tel Aviv String Quartet to the Fairmont Hotel. All of the money collected was supposed to go to the Jewish National Fund (JNF). I think it's the first example of the JNF refusing to take money from somebody. We had to give the check anonymously to the Jewish Welfare Federation because there was such hostility from the JNF. I thought that the great bridge we had with the Jewish community was the Soviet Jewry issue, because we're concerned about that, and many groups in the Bay Area are concerned about that. We sent volunteers to help Soviet Jewry groups in San Francisco. Of course, our people are all energetic and out to really accomplish something. One of the problems in the Jewish community is the need for volunteers. Our people went as volunteers and the Jewish community was completely convinced that we wanted to take over. We had a tremendous back-lash. So we withdrew from any active public involvement. We felt that on a one-to-one level we could have good relations with the Jewish community.

I started the Creative Community Project five years ago. I felt that there were many professionals in the Bay Area who not only did not want to involve themselves in any church, especially the Unification Church, and who didn't want to talk about God directly, but who wanted to live in a healthy community, a community with high ethical ideals. The great attraction of the Principle for me—and I came after studying it for a long while and looking at the people—was that it brought back my whole sense of the ethics of Judaism. For me, Judaism is essentially an ethical religion. The value I see in it is as an ethical tradition. When I came to the Unification Church, it was like, "There it is again." I had lost it somehow over the years. Buber had gotten me into all kinds of mystical things, like Hasidism, and somehow the practical ethics of community got lost somewhere. For me, the ethics of community are very important. I had a lot of friends who could not relate to the church, but who could relate to an ethical community of creative people working together. A number of professors who taught at U.C. Berkeley and other places would later move into our community, the Creative Community Project. They just wanted to be members of a community that was living a high ethical life. That was our purpose and at the same time it created a bridge for people who wanted to get involved in the Unification Church. What we wanted to do was involve people in a movement that was dedicated to making real God's ideal in the world. It seemed to me that everything Rev. Moon represented was to create projects that could relate to people. So the Creative Community Project was another way that I dreamed up, with a few other people who help me, of translating how I could reach professional people. That was the original idea.

In the Bay Area we also have the Unification Church, we have the MFT,* we have CARP, we have tables, as some of you know, in the Civic Center and Fisherman's Wharf where people say, "Hi! We're the Moonies. You've heard about us, but how much do you know about us?" We've got those tables, our MFT people wear little badges that say "Unification Church," others invite people to lectures. There are many ways in which we reach people.

---

*A group of mobile fund-raising teams that raise money for the Unification Church.

Basically, however, I have felt that the way you communicate a religious idea to someone is as much by listening as by talking. I am on the streets witnessing maybe four hours a day. But what I do is I attempt to make a basis of relationship with someone. I see someone with a book. It may be by Ken Kesey. I teach literature. How do you make a relationship with someone? You go up and say, "Hi! How do you like that book?" You start a conversation. Realistically, that person is going to get on the bus in four minutes. I don't know if you've ever witnessed on the street and tried to invite someone over to your house in four minutes, but this is my existentialist frame. I've got four minutes to establish a credible, loving, trusting relationship with this person. My motivation is to find a way to give God's love to this person, to establish a relationship that we can build on. I may only have a chance to get this person's address so that I can call for coffee later on. I may only tell him later on that I am the director of the Unification Church in the Bay Area, and the director of the Creative Community Project and that I teach at Laney College, etc. My initial impulse is to establish a relationship. Once I've got a relationship, then I can explain a lot of other things. Who wants to talk about ontology and eschatology unless you happen to be really involved in those areas? I talk to a lot of people about the Yankees. I can make a good basis there. I can go way back on Yankee stuff. I've got down all the figures on the Yankees. I can bring more people to the Unification Church by starting out with the Yankees. It is all a matter of relationship. I don't want to lay a trip on anybody. I teach all our people first to establish a relationship, and not to lay a trip on anybody, not to kill anybody by shoving on them your insight or religious idealism. Understand where people are coming from. Listen to their heart. Listen to their ideas. Listen to their dreams, their aspirations, their hopes. Try to establish a positive basis of relationship so that you can follow up on it. That's the basic way of relating.

Project Volunteer is another project that deals with social service to the community. I teach at Laney—Laney is an inner-city college. It has mostly black, brown and oriental people. I came there in the '60s when it was an example of a multi-racial urban campus. I was interested in the anti-war movement, and it was the home of the anti-war movement, outside of Cal-Berkeley. Laney College: that was where it was at. I was always interested in community things. I'm on the Oakland Committee for Aging, I was on the Oakland Committee for Economic Development. I'm involved with community. So as an extension of this, what do I do? I create a Project Volunteer that can serve the community. All of our literature says: "Associated with and independent of the Unification Church." We work now with about 100 groups throughout the State. Everybody knows from our literature that we're Unification Church, but we don't go up to someone and say, "Look. We want to give you food. We're from the Unification Church." We say, "Look. We are from Project Volunteer. Here's our literature to read if you want to read it and find out all about us. Our purpose is to serve the community and neighborhood. We're going to ship food to Zaire, if you want to come down and bring your volunteers to help us load it on the train, fine." It's all out there. Our desire is to serve a purpose. If they want to know our background, they can. If they involve themselves at all with us, it's all out there so that they can see what they are involving themselves with. It's true that three years ago we did not have on our evening program form the full outline of the Unification Church and its background. As soon as it was brought to our attention that this was a difficulty, we changed. Anybody who comes over to our centers or has any involvement with us at all, knows it's directly connected with the Unification Church. If they come to the Church directly, there's no problem. For every seminar that anyone goes to, a person must sign a form that indicates that it's a project sponsored by the Unification Church.

But we are constantly criticized in the media for not announcing immediately that we are Moonies. But when I'm witnessing, in my heart I'm saying, "Heavenly Father, how can I find Your long-lost children? How can You use me as an instrument of Your love. The world is suffering." I give lectures every night. Most people do not have the foggiest idea of ethics at all. Especially young people. They don't have any idea about it. I feel that if I just give them an ethical framework in which to think about ethical questions, it's valuable, whether or not they come to a seminar, involve themselves with the Church or anything. I feel an obligation as God's son to serve my brothers and sisters, to give them something of value. If they then want to pursue that, then there are all kinds of ways to do that.

How do you lecture to people? You can't just lecture,

"Believe this or die." At least you can't from my framework. My background in literature says that you must please people to teach people. So you have to make instruction funny, you have to give them Jewish humor from New York. You give them anything that will make them laugh, because if you just give them something like, "OK, here's the Truth, and this is going to be good for you, take it or die," nobody's going to receive that. Who wants to work for the goodness of the world? Everybody is looking for self-benefit, so if you can make him see that self-benefit is connected with the goodness of the world, great. So when people come over at night, they have a wonderful experience. Everybody in our family, in our Church in the Bay Area, says, "Look, you must give God's love and God's truth to the people. Truly serve them. You be God, you act as Jesus Christ to these people. What would you do if you were Jesus, and you had these people for two hours? How would you serve them, how would you love them, how would you care for them? Be like God to these people." So they have a tremendous loving experience. They're in an environment where everybody's loving them, caring for them. They may think, "Wow, this is far out. This is really kooky." They may think this is something special. So they come to a seminar, and they are really loved, because we are trying to think about role-playing God.

The central core of the Unification Church teaching and practice is to develop God-centered love. The thing that I have learned in the Unification Church is that the way in which I can resemble God most is through my heart, developing God's heart, and taking responsibility in my heart for other human beings. So everybody is trained to develop God's heart.

How well do we do it? We carry with us all the old baggage from wherever we came from, but at least everybody is thinking about, "How can I give God's love, God's heart, to my guest, my friend, my mom and dad, my neighbor, my uncle, whoever is at the seminar." And they genuinely have a transforming experience. They are loved like they've never been loved in their whole life. People genuinely care for their guests. They think, "This is my child, and I am God. Here is my son or daughter whom I have been missing for 6000 years. I have to serve this person with everything I've got. I may be tired, I may have a cold, it doesn't matter." Why do the people in the Church inspire me? Because I see that even when they are sick, they are out there, completely for other people. That for me was Christ's love, and it transformed my whole life to know what that meant.

So, people have a tremendous experience. They're loved up: they're given the way, the truth and the life and the love, imitations of Christ. That's the path they are shown. Once they've received that love, they feel real good. Then after two days or seven days or 21 days, they realize, "Uh, oh. I have to start giving it back." In other words, they come back into the city, and they go back to school, or back to work, or whatever they're doing with their life. And there is the crisis point in their spiritual life, because they realize, "My goodness, I've got to take responsibility for my own life. I've got to create this ideal." That's the transition to mature spiritual life, the beginning of the journey for a lot of people.

Some people have their faith broken. When they are kidnapped they are told, "The people didn't love you, don't you see, it was all just a nice environment, everybody was singing 'You are my sunshine,' you were looking at the Golden Gate Bridge, and that's what did it. It was just everybody making believe that they were loving you and you were never loved before and you are only 23 and you are on a journey and blah, blah." The critics focus on all the external reasons why people change. Even though those things are true, they were genuinely offered God's love and a way of life that for me is the central core of Judaeo-Christian tradition. The Principle is not some weird, freaky idea; it's the core of my Jewish experience, and the core of what I have studied of Christianity. But it means taking it seriously 24 hours a day.

I was an existentialist-Marxist before I came to the Unification Church, so for me the idea of taking responsibility for every thought, every feeling, every action, was liberating — because I knew I had to do it. There was a framework of absurdity in which I had to do it — Sisyphus pushing the rock up the hill. All of a sudden I had a kind of responsibility which was complete and total, for everything: the way you look at someone, the way you move, the way you fall on the ground. If you fall on the ground, do it with grace, do it with a sense of purpose, with beauty . . .

Many people have been deeply moved by their experience here. But sometimes, even from within the Church, we get persecution; some say we in Northern California are horizontal while everybody else in the movement is vertical in orientation.

That's the most ridiculous thing I have ever heard. How can you possibly love people all the time unless you're centered on God? If you weren't you'd just get wiped out. You couldn't possibly do it. We're probably the most orthodox Moonies in the whole world because we believe you have to be joyful and give God's love when you are hurting. That's the difficult part. To actually extend to people and witness on the streets when your back hurts, and to give God's love when you can't even talk, that's really being out there for people. It's very exhilarating, too, when people get into it. "Wow, this is really exciting, this is incredible. We *are* revolutionaries! We *are* going to build the Kingdom, today! In fact, this *is* the Kingdom." Sometimes, even people in our Church are overwhelmed. "These people really believe they are creating the Kingdom!" In other words, we often have leaders who have been in the Church a long time, who think, "Well, the Kingdom is way out there " or "There's a symbolic Kingdom, and maybe someday." We believe God is creating the Kingdom now, tonight, this moment! And every moment, we have to make it sacred. If you look at brothers and sisters, you have to treat them as God. We absolutely cannot tolerate anything else but that. If you're spacing out, you should know that you're spacing out. You can do it if you want to, but take responsibility for it. So it becomes a very responsible life. People for the first time in their life, think, "Religion isn't a space-out, it is a love-in." And all of a sudden, Wow! You've got to take complete responsibility for acting like Christ each moment. It sets in motion all kinds of things. A young member will call his parents at home and say, "Gee, Mom and Dad. I just discovered Christianity. Why didn't you tell me all my life? You're a minister, where are you at?" The people we get, as Dr. Judah knows, are often people who come from good families and yet there is a vacuum, that big hole and then something happens. They don't find in the culture the reinforcement of very old values. So we give it to them.

Neil Duddy: I'm really glad to hear you say that you are a servant to the people in the Bay Area. I'm especially pleased that you are supporting and encouraging service, having folks in the Unification movement see themselves as servants of Christ, as His agents and models of transformation. I'm particularly glad to hear you say it because of your position here in the Unification Church.

But there are still some problems. As recently as November 1978 I know of two people who went across the Berkeley campus and were approached by folks supporting the Creative Community who, when asked if it was associated with the Unification Church, refused to answer. In the fall, also, there were a couple of folks out near College Avenue soliciting funds in wheelchairs. But they really didn't have any injury. In talking to them they just said that being out and soliciting funds for the Church is a hard job and the "wheelchairs help us avoid blisters on our feet." That is rather difficult to appreciate. I think that these kinds of incidents serve as points of fixation for people in the media. The media attaches itself to things that can create stigmas very easily. They are things that are visible, things that are titillating, things that are fascinating and things that should be avoided.

Darrol Bryant: (to Mose Durst) Do you know about this?

Neil Duddy: I was in Boston three weeks ago, and the same incident occurred out there. After talking with them for about five minutes and pursuing it further, I could determine they were members of the Unification Church. It was very touchy, and I realized the volatile nature of it.

Mose Durst: There are people in the Church who do fund-raise in wheelchairs. The reason for that is, at least for the ones I know of, that their legs *actually* hurt, and they do have medical problems. I have fund-raised and one of the most existential experiences in my life is going 16 hours on the streets with two bunches of roses in my hands and asking people to buy them. When you are walking up to them your whole life flashes in front of you. You begin wondering why you're here. And if you go many hours a day, day in and day out, you start hurting, you really start hurting. Everybody here who is a member of the Church has fund-raised. A lot of people do have problems with their legs, and I know that even when they get into wheelchairs, usually they'll sit in parking lots or places like that. I wish there were some easier way to make money for the Church. In the older churches there are tithings and ways in which the established members of the community can fund church causes. I've been in the Fairmont Hotel when a million dollars for the United Jewish Fund was raised in a few minutes. I was invited to hear our Israeli diplomat. He gave a little talk for 30 minutes, and after he finished explaining the crisis in Israel, which we all knew about anyway, they brought out the Israel bonds. In about 30 minutes they collected a million dollars. Everybody there was just obliged. The reason they were invited was that they were expected to give x thousands of dollars to the Jewish Fund.

Unfortunately, our movement is young in America, and to do the kinds of things that we do, we are willing to put ourselves on the line. My wife was an early missionary here. She worked at two jobs, she lectured, she was the only person when she came to Oakland, and she founded the Oakland Unification Church by herself. She had tuberculosis for a year as well as numerous other sicknesses. Her story is just like the missionaries of all the great religions. It was only after the foundation was built that something substantial could happen. But back to the wheelchair business: people should identify themselves and they should only use wheelchairs if there is a real need, not for some kind of phony reason.

Neil Duddy: In talking with the woman we simply tried to tell her what our response was and to encourage her to take a day off, that God's grace really couldn't find its fullness in her stressful situation. She needed a day off. Or she should go out and get a different job so that she could strengthen her legs a bit. The amount of empathy drawn by folks soliciting funds from wheelchairs and things of that nature borders closely on deception. Conversely, it's interpreted by the solicitor as a tremendous act demonstrating spirituality and an attempt to accomplish God's Kingdom.

Mose Durst: One of the greatest problems that I find is that our leadership is often so young. It would be nice if they came in at the age of thirty of forty, as I came in. One of the great frustrations for me is that people in our own movement do not understand the depth or the comprehensiveness of the Principle. They're looking for a savior, they're looking for something to get high on, they're looking for something and don't realize that Christianity is a really big, heavy, deep thing. It's going to change their whole life, and they have to develop a great maturity to deal with the largeness of Jesus Christ. So they do all kinds of things that are just shocking to me. Let me give you an example. Daphne Greene is one of the great critics of the Church. Before her son came into the Church, we knew everything about him. We knew he was on drugs, we knew he was an unstable guy, we knew he was going to cause a lot of potential problems, but what was our option? Well, we've got to give God's love to everybody. Welcome Mr. Greene. It's like Jesus—when Judas betrayed him, it wasn't the first time. It couldn't have been the first time. Jesus must have known where Judas was at. He must have betrayed him many times. But what was Jesus' option? All He could do was love him. That is what we are about: developing loving hearts and that is risky.

There are people in the movement who are completely off the page with Rev. Moon. Rev. Moon is trying to love the people, serve the people, anything, bend over backwards and do flips to make people comfortable. He's scrupulous in every activity. And here people do all these off-the-page activities. Even me. I wish that we could, in one sense, brainwash the members, in the sense that we could tell somebody to do something and ask them to please do it carefully. It's incredible what people will do. Our bookkeeper forgot to pay a mortgage on a property for five months. How could he forget to pay the thing for five months? In another house there is this balloon payment of the mortgage. How could you forget to read the contract? I lost some of my hair before the Church, but I've lost a lot more since the Church.

Millions of things come up that I would never have realized. I'm responsible for dealing with the media. We have a project at Booneville and much of the persecution here in California started about five years ago when NBC did a hatchet job on us. They flew over Booneville and took pictures of a barbed wire fence. There's about 50 feet of barbed wire on 700 acres at Booneville. It's an old sheep ranch. You couldn't lock the place in if you wanted to. The National Guard couldn't secure the place. Anyway, they took pictures of the barbed wire, and they blocked out the back so it looked like a concentration camp. The film was aired on NBC and made us look like real zombies. Before this film we'd never had a gate in Booneville, nothing was there. People could just come in and out. We had good relations with the neighbors. The film was shown on Thursday and, sure enough, starting on Friday night all the joy-riders from Cloverdale and Ukiah and Santa Rosa decided, "Let's go and harrass the Moonies." Beer cans were thrown all over the place, people started coming into the seminar, people started stealing the tools in the barn. So what do we do? Smart people that we are, we put up a gate, saying,

"No Trespassing." That's all we needed to do. Sunday morning in the *Chronicle,* here's the next Moonie headline, "No Trespassing Gate!" What a foreboding and forbidding place! It was kind of stupid of us to do that, obviously, and not to figure that it was going to lead to more complications. One thing like that leads to another. Dealing with media, learning how to smile when they have the cameras on you, teaching our people on the street how to speak to people. Those are the difficulties.

Matthew Morrison: On the wheelchair issue, I know that when I was directing fund-raising in Los Angeles, it was brought to the attention of Mr. Salonen who is president of the American Unification Church. He issued a state-wide bulletin that no one was allowed, unless they had casts on their legs, to use wheelchairs. I had a member who had a broken leg, and he was forbidden to use a wheelchair.

Mose Durst: When I came to the "family," or the "family" came to me, I had a big house in Piedmont and people just moved into my house. There were just a few members in our Church at that time in Oakland. What was the process of raising money? Everything was run loosely. I got my paycheck from school and it went into a common pot. Whoever needed money, used it. It's a family. I wasn't worried about tax-exemption. I was a Marxist-existentialist professor, so who is worried about a deduction from the government? You just gave whatever you had. One guy was going to Cal, and I gave him his expenses. Someone else got some money from a relative and they just threw it into the pot. If we could send money back East to help the national Church, we did. Actually, that was a priority. Everybody was like brothers and sisters living in a family. When it was an emergency, you helped out. Your car was anybody's car.

Then as we grew we had to develop books, records, receipts and a formal accounting system. Try being a Moonie and get auto insurance, that's an interesting one. You ought to try it sometime. It's impossible to get auto insurance that isn't outrageously expensive for our five vans. Nobody will insure you. Now we have an organization; it's a huge organization with insurance and buildings and property and other things. Here I am, a literature professor, worried about car insurance, and liability insurance and land, how to deal with the media and the sewer system that is polluting the well of the next-door neighbor.

All of these things are just incredibly complicated. Even with the best intentions, things bring about complexity without our wanting them to. And when things go wrong it takes years to straighten them out.

Take our bad image with the media. Take for instance somebody not identifying himself as a Church member. A number of people, when they begin witnessing are gun-shy. They're afraid to talk to anybody. It's not easy to go up to anybody on the street and stop them and start talking. People will think you're funny, some will abuse you, it happens every day. It's difficult. I've done it for years, and it's difficult. It's not easy going up to somebody and starting a conversation, especially for a young person who may be shy. But we encourage everybody: "Do you love God? Well, you have to care for people. You have to speak to them, bring them. We have to establish a foundation for our movement." Who's going to bring the members so they can go to the Seminary and go to all these places. We have a seminary, hospitals in Japan—where do the personnel come from? We bring them from the streets. How do we bring them? You have to talk to people. But it's not easy. So especially with all the persecution going on, people become extra shy. Then they wouldn't say anything if someone would ask, "Are *you* a member of the Unification Church?"—"Oh, no, not me, I was just walking down the street." We give so many talks to people: "Please identify yourself." At the very least, deception is counterproductive. Anything you do will come out in the open. Anything you do, whether it be in your closet or wherever, you've got to assume it's a public act. Every private act has public implications. And it's counterproductive in the most basic way either to try and deceive people or to try and say you are not who you are.

It's true, we've had to learn practical things, like writing on every form exactly who we are. If people sign up for a seminar, they know about the Church. You have to get it all out in black and white. At first we didn't do that. So there was a certain process. We didn't feel people were committing themselves to anything, they were just coming to a seminar. Later all these things got heavy in the press with accusations of our not being willing to cross our t's and dot our i's. But it's been a real process of learning. For me one of the most valuable things is to have healthy critics. When Dr. Frederick Sontag came up and went to our seminar, he gave us all kinds of advice. We followed everything he suggested, including clearly writing on the forms the name of the Church. With Project Volunteer, we made it clear from the very beginning that it was sponsored by the Church. But it took time for us to learn those things.

Darrol Bryant: Isn't it true that a fairly high percentage of people come into the Church through the Bay Area?

Mose Durst: Well, we like to think we get a few.

Virginia Hearn: Could you tell us what an average workshop is like?

Mose Durst: Our members will meet someone on the street and invite them over to have dinner. It's a warm environment. Then we have entertainment. The idea is that through music, song and a heavenly environment we can open a person's heart so that they can be receptive to new ideas. We believe that the heart is the way to the mind. Love is the basis by which you know something. To know something is to love something, and to love something is to be open to knowledge. We have dinner and entertainment, then I'll give a very brief talk which is an overview of the Principle. We will invite people to either a one or two day seminar. One of the ways that we bring in a number of people is that we have one day seminars every day, 365 days a year in every center. Every day it is at the same time: at six o'clock we have dinner, 6:45 the entertainment, 7:15 the lecture begins and at 9:00 the bus goes up to the land. This happens every night, 365 days a year. It's like business. If you want to make a successful business, you open the store at 7 a.m. and you close it at midnight. You're bound to hit a certain number of customers. But we are not looking to collect members. We're looking to transform our own lives by loving someone else. Our basic belief is that the best way to transform ourselves is by helping someone else grow in God's love.

Today is a holiday for us. It's the Day of All Things. After I left the conference last night, our "family" had a pledge service where we rededicated ourselves to God. We went to our Holy Ground in San Francisco and prayed for the Bay Area and the State of California. We came back at 2:30 in the morning. That was the beginning of our day, it's our way of praying for the whole area.

So anyway, they come to the evening program. Then they can go to a one or a two day seminar. The seminar will begin in the morning. They will wash in the morning, have exercises, breakfast, each will share a little bit about his or her life. There will be a lecture at 11 o'clock which will last about an hour. We believe in lectures that are short enough that people can tolerate them. Another part of our belief is that people have an attention span of 45 minutes to an hour for a serious lecture. After that we have a group meeting where people discuss the lecture and bring out various points. The group leader will seek to discuss certain key points in the lecture. No matter what way the discussion goes, the ideal is at least to bring out those key points and deal with them. The purpose of our seminar is to show each individual that he's a child of God, that it's possible to build a world that reflects God's love, and we hope that these people, by seeing us as examples of people who are working to develop God's love, can have hope for their lives. So we seek to give hope, love and life to people in that day. That is our purpose. We believe that you've got to give people hope, and you've got to give them joy by teaching them a way in which they can transform their lives and transform the world around them.

Then we have lunch. Then they play dodge ball. They jump up and down, it's very enthusiastic. We use the dodge ball or the kick ball or the volley ball as an example, as a means by which to show a person that the degree to which he actually participates in an experience determines what he gets out of it. It's a very revealing activity about a person and his way of being in the world. There are people who are just sort of hiding in the background. There are people who avoid the game, saying, "Well, it's too violent." Some say, "Well, I like to watch other people do it." Many things come out in that kind of game. It's an incredible learning experience. We do that, then we have wash-up or whatever, then there's another lecture at 4:00 on the Fall. The first lecture was on the Principle of Creation. There's a group meeting after the second lecture. The third lecture is about 5:30 and it's on Restoration, or the Mission of Jesus. Then there is dinner and later there will be entertainment. The process of entertainment is to create a skit or a song to try and exemplify in some concrete way what they've learned during the day. It's not just hearing words. The idea of the day is to act in such a way as to make the ideas real. The day should be a transforming experience. In the evening then, we have entertainment and it's usually a very moving experience. Then at 10:00 we have a final sharing of what the day was like for each one. If it's a two-day seminar, we ask, "What do you look forward to for tomorrow?" We try to encourage people to take responsibility and set goals. People go to sleep at 11:00.

The staff of the seminar then evaluates each person: How is this person? What does he need? Where is he coming from? What are his values and his ideals? What did you learn from him? What can we teach him? What does he need tomorrow? How were the people in your group? Were the family members really responsible for other people, or were they just spacing out? What was the relationship of the words which we spoke to the actions which we were doing? For me, the evening lecture is a prayer. It's a check on my day. I see to what degree I'm living the words that are coming out of my mouth. So the lectures on the weekend are not just meant to be heard over and over again. They are meant to grow another human being: to see to what degree you're living your own ideals. We use it as a check on our own lives, an alignment, a spiritual alignment. So that's how we end the day. Usually the whole thing is a very moving experience. Even if people disagree with all the ideas, they realize, "Well, they're good people, and I wish them well."

We have a bus that goes down every night. Those people who want to leave get on the bus and go home. People who want to stay — we encourage people to stay — stay. They might stay for two, seven, or 21 days. Then they will come back into the city and participate in some way in the life of the city. We have people of all sorts: engineers, professors, doctors, young people. One of the unique features of the Bay Area is that we do have people who work at a full-time or a part-time job, or go to school and have normal lives. We have that kind of flexibility, and we find that it draws more people to our movement here to have that range of activities that a person can do. It gives us a basis of relating to almost everybody in the community. Our Project Volunteer, our Professional Society, and our Neighborhood Program are three programs that reach everybody in the community. They reach throughout the State of California.

In case you are wondering, about 15% of our people support the other 85%. In other words we minimize fund-raising. It's true that the 15% that do fund-raising go out for two or three weeks and work real hard. When they come back, another group goes out and they raise the money that supports the other 85% of the people. The reason for that is that we find it's more important to bring people than to bring money. You can't do the activities unless you pay the mortgages and bills. I don't know if you've ever been involved in running a church, but to pay the bills on x number of properties, and vehicles and health care and all the other expenses that a member has—and we pay everything—is a big task. Unless they've got a rich uncle or aunt or a parent who's willing to pay it we pay it. Most people will not ask their parents.

Virginia Hearn: Do you ever charge people?

Mose Durst: We charge everybody who comes to our seminar $20 for the weekend and $50 for the week. We used to try and give the seminars free, but it was counterproductive. People got nothing out of it. They felt, "Well, I'm getting it for free, it's not worth anything." So we charge everybody. Everybody who comes to our programs has to pay because we feel that we are giving a professional service. Our image, our activities and our functions are as professional as anything I've ever been involved in. We are professionals, we give a very professional seminar. They are going to get their money's worth. EST charges $300. We charge $20 for the weekend or $50 for the week.

Virginia Hearn: I have a lot of admiration for that kind of dynamic, but what motivates you? In the years of your commitment to the church, have you ever found that in spite of your good intentions your selfish cussedness comes to the fore and in a given relationship or relationships, you have really been hurtful, perhaps seriously hurtful? If so, what is your response to that?

Mose Durst: Well, that has certainly happened. It probably happens every day. My wife, thank God, is the kind of person who upholds the standard that before the sun sets, everything must be cleared. Although we have hurt each other, the Principle that we live by is a redemptive principle. Christ loves a redemptive life. We are here to love each other, not to judge each other or to hurt each other, although we may do a lot of judging and a lot of hurting. That's real, and that is our life. We are in a growth process. The only thing that saves me, personally—and it's in my relationship to my wife—is that standard where before we hit the sack, before we put our heads on the pillow, we get on our knees and pray and make sure that our hearts are clear. The most beautiful thing in my life is when we wake up in the morning at 5 o'clock, and my wife and I get down on our knees and pray to God that God can guide us through the day, so that we might be of service to Him. When we go to sleep at night, we get down on our knees and pray that we have helped Him in some way, and that our hearts are unburdened in our love for each other, in our love for the "family," our love for the world, and our love for God. That's the only thing that allows me to renew my day. When I teach my classes, sometimes I'm short with a student. I may be impatient. So each day I must go into my office and close the door and pray that God will forgive me and allow me to be tolerant to my students, allow me to be open to them and to listen to them, not just to the words they speak, but to their hearts and soul. But I have my shortcomings and I don't always do that. But my great hope and my great joy is that I believe in a redemptive Lord. I've experienced it, I've seen it work. It's the only way out of what I see as the tragedy of human life. Rev. Moon has a famous speech called "Victory Over Resentment." As I've experienced the world, everybody has been hurt by life and everybody hurts others, and everybody therefore has some reason to resent the world, be bitter about something. The only way out is that divine love, that redemptive love, Christ's love.

Virignia Hearn: And if someone comes to you and says, "How come you're so different?" what do you say?

Mose Durst: Well, ultimately I try to explain to him that I try to live by ideals. It's the ideal that is transforming my life. All that I can share with them is my ideal and my person. I'm a unique person as is everyone else. If you get to know people in the Unification Church you will find that the more they're involved in the Church the more unique they are. The people I know are the most unique batch of people I've ever met. If you share a common ideal, it allows you to trust that you can be unique. For example, if we share a common ideal, it allows us to be vulnerable. If you love your husband and he loves you, you share an ideal in common. You can be vulnerable and make mistakes. He's not going to slam you. He may say, "Darling, you've made a terrible mistake, let me help you." There's a heart of love, even if he wants to correct you. So the same thing applies to the world. We can become more unique and vulnerable, if we share an ideal or a value that can embrace the depth of the self and the depth of the other. If we can truly respect the other in the most fundamental way, see divinity in the other, even if that person is not acting divinely, then we are developing a heart of love. It's real, it's not an illusion. Underneath that rough exterior there is a divine soul, and that's what we have to relate to. Why do we smile all the time? Because we are trying to relate to God within ourselves and to the God within others. Even though we, like everyone else, feel a whole range of emotions—anger, frustration, whatever—the question is, what do we do with our emotions? In the 60's you could just dump everything out on somebody else and feel, "Well, now I'm authentic." Real authenticity for us is the alignment of our individual feeling with a deeper purpose. It's a relationship that is important to us—to other people, to God—and the redemptive love that guides the relationship.

Virginia Hearn: To what do you attribute the animosity of ex-members?

Mose Durst: I, for one, have really tried to explore that because it's been so painful to me. They are often people I've loved and lived with. It's been the most baffling experience of my whole life. I think it has to do with the betrayal of love which is always painful, and the betrayal of love with such viciousness is just an added dimension of pain. Let me try to explain what I mean. I believe that in our movement people have genuinely experienced love, often it's a love that they never experienced before. And when they are somehow led to believe, for whatever reasons, that the love was false, they are very angry. Usually this process is one of breaking their faith. The same love that was directed in a constructive way, now, all of a sudden, becomes this lashing out, this hate. Literally it's hate, that's all it is. It's a desire to inflict pain on the object that you once loved. That's one dynamic that goes on.

In addition, people feel very bitter if they come to believe that they have been betrayed in love, that it isn't real, that it was all phony. They feel manipulated: my love was abused. I think that's the sense that many people have when they've had their faith broken, when they come to distrust what they had experienced in the "family." I think it's tragic that they come to feel that way. My experience of people who have dropped out, the ones who have become really vicious against the Church, it's like they never were here, ever! Of all the things they had experienced here they don't seem to remember any. It's like it never existed. This is another thing that I do not understand to this day, how can that happen? Their way of life afterwards is often an indication that nothing ever happened when they were here.

But basically, I see the animosity of former members as a

dynamic revolving around the betrayal of love. There are other kinds of subsidiary things, but that's the main thing. People feel betrayed. They feel that they were manipulated, that they were abused, that the ideals that they were hopeful about and felt were real, really were not real, that the people they trusted and loved so much were really trying to deceive them. I think that it would be very painful to feel that way. But, fortunately I don't feel that way. I'm not worried. What Rev. Moon has done for me is to give me a basis for dealing with life in a much more profound and beautiful way. Even if, God forbid, he is storing up bucks in Tarrytown, I hope that my love is deep enough to redeem him, because he's given me a tremendous desire to deal in a loving way with difficult problems. I would think that people who feel that in some manner we have abused them would seek in some way to redeem us. They don't. They want to destroy us with a passion. That's what I don't understand. There is no desire to have real, honest dialogue. Of all the people who have been kidnapped—and that's really the only way that people have turned against us, people have left our family here who say we're OK, but they simply "can't do it"—no one has ever come back and sat down with me and explained what was wrong, or what their new experience was; no one has ever come back or confronted me directly over all the years.

Lewis Rambo: How many would you estimate that number to be?

Mose Durst: I would say that in all the years I've been here there must have been about 40 people who have been kidnapped, and not one has ever come back to sit down with me and explain what happened.

Neil Duddy: Was Christopher Edwards here?

Mose Durst: Yes. Here's a person who had a very difficult time loving people. He came from a very wealthy east coast family. He went to Yale, was very intellectual, but completely unable to love. He was on a lot of drugs when he came here. He hadn't been living with his parents when he came here. He lived with a couple who were doing, ironically as it turns out, these mind control experiments. It is curious, almost funny, that almost all the things that people accuse us of are usually things that they have been involved with in their own lives. Here's a guy who, for the most part, ran his own show. He was a tutor to the children, he was working on establishing a school. He read all the books he

wanted to read. He had done a study on Hegel when he was at
Yale, so we'd have all these discourses on Hegel. Our relationship
was very intellectual. He read everything and basically did whatever
he wanted to do. He wasn't really a solid member because he
couldn't take the normal schedule of our life. So he lived in our
professional house on Regent Street and actually followed pretty
much his own schedule. He was not under any pressure at all.

But what happened was that his dad came to Hearst Street
house to a lecture. Afterwards, we asked him if he had any
questions. "No," he replied with this bright smile, and bright
eyes. He loved everything. "Oh, everything was wonderful, I'm so
happy my son is here." The next day Jessica—the girl who served
us hors d'oeuvres earlier—and Chris were in the car. Ted Patrick
and his goon squad took Jessica and threw her ten feet out of the
car, stole her purse and grabbed Chris Edwards by the hands and
feet, and threw him kicking and screaming into a van with bars
on it.

That's the last we saw of him. That was the end of Chris
Edwards; we never heard from him again. Then we heard that he
was involved back East with others trying to break people's faith.
The guy had a lot of problems in being able to love people. He
experienced a genuine love and it moved him very deeply. When
he was taken—I know the process that Patrick puts people
through—his love and his ideals and his faith were broken. So he
came to believe, somehow, that his experience was all betrayal, it
was all false. Everybody was singing, "You are my Sunshine" and
talking about the heavenly Kingdom and all that. It's such a
cheap caricature. It's like spiritual pornography. Like being a
pickpocket and going up to saints and only seeing their pockets.
That's the level the book is at: a prostitute looking at the St.
Francis Hotel and seeing everybody as a potential customer.
That's the kind of sensibility that book comes from. He was a
very delicate person who was just beginning to blossom.

Darrol Bryant: How long had he been here?

Mose Durst: A few months. Most of the time he was still into
his own schedule. He was very egoistic. He wasn't that special, by
our standards, but he said he was. He went to Yale so he put a lot
of emphasis on that. Actually, all the people we get here are
pretty sharp. Christina is Phi Beta Kappa at Cal, Mike has got all
these keys, many that join our movement have degrees and
awards and keys. We could melt down the Phi Beta Kappa keys

and fill up a trunk. He wasn't unique. We get pretty high level people.

What we do with everybody is to determine, "What can he do, what does he like to do? How can we broaden him out?" We saw that Chris was interested in education, so we let him work on a school. We tried to really grow him, to let him do his thing. We tried to draw him out gradually and to let him see that he's responsible to other people. It's a process. Our style out here is that we try to deal very individually with each person. We have to let them unfold. Each person is very unique, and we try to baby everybody. Sometimes we let people do things that are completely selfish and off the page, but they are just growing.

Darrol Bryant: I think that your response to Professor Rambo's question is a partial one in the sense that it offers a kind of psychological explanation about why people become the way they become when they go through deprogramming. But there is another dimension to the whole phenomenon that is related to some socio-political forces in our society. Let me give you an example. I came here and went through the weekend up at Camp K. It was a very interesting experience for me, and a deeply moving one. The only thing you forgot to mention in your description of Camp K was how much they sing on the weekend. I hadn't sung so much in the past half-dozen years of my life put together, as I did in that weekend. Anyway, after that I went back to Canada, and not more than a month later, I had a call from a woman from the Canadian Broadcasting Company (CBC) who subsequently came out here to California. She was working for *The Fifth Estate,* a CBC public affairs program. They have an hour show once a week, and it's usually half an hour on one subject and half an hour on another. It has, I think, a fairly good reputation. The CBC has, for me, an extremely good reputation. I think of it as a tremendous system, and they do very, very fine work. She was interested in doing something on new religions, and had seen my name somewhere or other, and wondered if she might talk with me. So she came out to Waterloo and met with me and Rod Sawatsky who has also been involved in the study of the Unification Church. We spent a day with her and gave her all kinds of material. We got all kinds of assurances from her about her concern to give a fair treatment of the movement. I gave her your name and Christina's name, and told her about my experience here and other people in the Unification movement that

I had met. She really traded in on that conversation with Rod and me in terms of making contact with various people. So they came out here and they did the show. And it was some show! It turned out not to be on the new religions, but specifically on the Unification Church. It presented the whole thing along the lines of ours being an age when people are seeking simple answers to complex questions. And one of the worst groups trading on this simple-mindedness is the Unification Church.

There had been an agreement that they might film Camp K. And Eric, the commentator on the show, posed as a person who happened to be on Fisherman's Wharf and was met by a member of the Unification Church. He went along to a Friday night meal and then the weekend. They showed a lot of things from Camp K, and what they showed was very fine. But they had to overlay it with a lot of commentary so that people wouldn't misunderstand what was going on. We saw people playing volley ball and listening to lectures and talking and singing and generally enjoying themselves. But the commentary said that there was something sinister going on here. Things weren't as they appeared to be. They also showed a Unification center not far from Toronto. But how did they shoot it? There's a barbed wire fence around this rural property. They shot the house on the hill through the barbed wire fence so that all you could really see is the barbed wire fence and the house is sort of indistinctly there in the background. It just blew me away. They interviewed several people on the show, but not one person who had any training in religious studies or theology. What's in it for those people to do that? They had never had any kind of relationship with the Unification Church. That's an additional part of the puzzle: the social forces that seem to be at work here to make it very, very important to discredit this movement, and show how terrible it is. I think you need to add a socio-political component to your understanding of what is happening.

Neil Duddy: We have had media come through, particularly since November, and they ask questions about different groups. It's very obvious from the beginning that they have a pre-set disposition. Some of that comes from the general backlash to a number of groups having, what we refer to as, an "esoteric gap." Some of the New Age religious movements have a habit of presenting themselves in a way that exposes as little as possible right in the beginning. They only present what is palatable and digestable. As the person makes more of a commitment, there is more knowledge given. When a person is about to move from being a disciple to becoming a teacher, he may find if he really evaluates the knowledge that he was initially taught and what he now knows about the entire commitment, that what he initially thought the group was about and what he now knows the group to be about are different. Things have become twisted. That can be a very disconcerting thing. We have to tell people that, yes, there are esoteric groups. But not everyone is in that category. Some people will tell you the story straight from the beginning. But with the media there is a big problem there. There's a tendency to assume that everything has an "esoteric gap" behind it, because some groups do. The group that I've been particularly studying spent $40,000 in the United States last year buying advertisements in different newspapers, giving what is a basic confession of Evangelical Christianity. It's just amazing, but what they really believe and how they practice it in their church has no resemblance to what they say they are in public. The media picks up on these discrepancies particularly when they are buying media time. A number of groups embody that type of process. So it is difficult for the media. It's very hard, when you do have a group that's being straight-forward, to convince the media to trust them, that that's what they really believe and there's nothing behind it.

Lewis Rambo: I don't know about the news media presentation, but I would say that this is a general problem in our society. How often have you seen a standard, conservative Christian group portrayed realistically? For example, in a film, it's generally a caricature of some kind or another. The preacher is usually put down either by the film or by the audience as somebody who is a demagogue.

Dagfinn Aslid: I used to work with the Norwegian radio, and I've done some free-lance journalism. I know the temptation to scandalize and dichotomize to portray something that has news value. It's very exciting to watch the revelation of what is really happening under the surface of things. I think that is quite an important factor in television in this country in the portrayal of religious groups. There seems to be a great need to play up the image of animosity between poor parents and victimized kid who has fallen prey to some sect.

Jonathan Wells: I wanted to make a theological point. It

concerns "heavenly deception" which I presume everyone here has heard about. It's often alleged that this is a practice of the Unification Church. It is not. The basis for the allegation is, I believe, found in the Unification account of Jacob's course in which the Bible says that Jacob deceived Esau. And not only that, but Rebecca deceived Isaac and there is a whole set of deception stories there. The Unification Church says that actually it was God's will that Jacob did what he did. I saw an evangelical version of the Jacob story on television a few months back which said exactly the same thing. Some claim, on this basis, that the Unification Church teaches its members to systematically deceive people. That is not true. Yet the allegation persists. I think the public has an almost subliminal conviction that the Unification Church in fact teaches "heavenly deception."

Lewis Rambo: Can I make a comment on that? I went to Bush Street one evening. I had been invited through Mike, so I knew what was going on. During the time I was there, God was mentioned once or twice and then very vaguely. If I were an 18 or 19 year-old kid just off the streets I would not have any idea what was going on. It just looks like nice people with great ideas that no one in their right mind could possibly disagree with. But Rev. Moon was never mentioned, Jesus Christ was never mentioned, religion was never mentioned, except for a vague, "Well, most of us came from religious backgrounds." So I think that is confusing for an outsider. In one sense, it is not deception. Indeed some Protestant denominations have religious surveys that are in fact recruitment efforts. But my point is that it's not totally groundless to claim that there is deception there. Maybe you're not taught to do that. But if someone doesn't know about the movement, it might take a couple of days to get the point of what the movement is about because Rev. Moon was never mentioned. I was very careful to watch for that because I was concerned about this issue. I wanted to get a fair picture. Is that deception or not? I didn't see those sign-up sheets. The night I was there, I don't think anyone signed one. There was a guest register that I signed when I came in. But I knew what it was, so I wasn't looking for anything there. But I consciously watched for mention of the Church, God, Jesus Christ, Moon. Were they ever mentioned? No. Now, that's not deception, but how does one justify that? I mean, obviously you don't dump everything in one night, but there is a big difference between dumping everything and dumping nothing. The things that were said were such vague generalities that everyone, unless they were imbeciles, would agree with them.

Now, I like Dr. Durst's point earlier about the ethical framework. That's a start. But ethics have ontological foundations upon which they are built. Now obviously you can't dump all that in one night. But I can see why somebody might say, "Hey, I just wanted to go up and have a nice time for the weekend, and on the third day I finally heard that Moon is behind this." At least, when I was a kid and went to Southern Baptist camps I knew that it was a Southern Baptist camp. I knew it wasn't just a fun weekend. And I don't see what you would lose by making it very clear in the first lecture what is going on a bit more explicitly.

Darrol Bryant: Can I make one comment? I was very intrigued by what Dr. Durst was saying tonight. In my impression what he's saying is that there's a real issue here as to what the real content of the movement is. You are predicating your question on the assumption that the real content is Rev. Moon and all the explicitly religious claims of this movement, but isn't Dr. Durst suggesting something else?

Lewis Rambo: One of the criticisms I have of evangelicals is that they are not always up-front about their activities. So I would make the same criticism of them. If you are raising money, if you are doing anything, don't go into a setting and pretend that you are not working for Bob Smith, or whoever you are raising money for. That is deception. And so I would say across the board, be very up-front. There's no reason for you not to be up-front. It seems to me that any movement that bases itself on honesty and integrity will come through in the end.

Stillson Judah: I wanted to interject something right here at this particular point. One of the things that's been very interesting to me is the early history of the Church in this particular area. Mike Mickler has been working on this early history and I've gotten a lot from him. We went together to see Mr. Choi who was also one of the early missionaries here in this area. Miss Kim was working here at the same time. But they each had entirely different methods. It seems to me that we have in the Creative Community Project a combination of two different methods. In talking with Mr. Choi, I discovered that he was not interested in the theology of the Unification Church, but in the carrying out of these principles in daily living. In other words, he was interested in love, caring and self-sacrifice. He didn't really care very much about the theology. His work in San Francisco went along these practical lines. He wrote a little book called *Principles of Education.*

Miss Kim, however, worked on an entirely different platform. She was interested in the theology. So, under her direction those who went out talked in terms of the theology of Rev. Moon and the whole Divine Principle. So you had these two different thrusts. It seems to me that what we have in the Creative Community Project is a combination of these two methods. When I went up to Booneville for the first weekend, I didn't hear anything about Rev. Moon either. But this seemed to be following exactly in the path that Mr. Choi had given. I understand that in the following week, one would get the theological side, which would represent the other side that had been given by Miss Kim. It seems to me that this is the way the thing really operated from the beginning. But the way it looks on the surface is, "Oh, well, this is 'heavenly deception' because you started off without mentioning that it was the Unification Church." I think that on that one weekend that I was up there, Rev. Moon's name wasn't mentioned at all.

Darrol Bryant: That was true in my experience, too.

Lewis Rambo: I'm not advocating that you present the whole theology at once. But at least you can make it clear where you are coming from. If for nothing else, you should do this for public relations.

Darrol Bryant: There are two points that I wanted to make. The first was to confirm what Dr. Durst said. When I went up to Camp K, I filled out a form that said, "The Creative Community Center is associated with and independent of the Unification Church." But there's another kind of point that I'm wanting to make here—this has just occurred to me tonight—but I don't know if I can articulate it clearly. But I'm trying to listen to what Dr. Durst is saying. I tend to be very sympathetic to the criticism being presented. But what I'm hearing Dr. Durst say is something like this: all dimensions of life are, in principle, open to God. Consequently, the way in which God is present in the world is not simply through theology or religion or the Church. These are not the only channels through which God is manifested in the world. If you begin with that assumption, it seems to make perfect sense that you would not necessarily mention anything of an explicitly religious or theological nature at a first meeting. Why not? Well, it is simply because that is not the only way in which one comes to have contact with the divine. One can begin anywhere, since everything is open to God.

Lewis Rambo: But that's a very abstract kind of argument. I think that in the actual practice of the way most people live their lives, people like things to be forthright. It's a very simple human desire. If you walk into a store, you want to know the name of the store. You want to know what you're buying. And I don't think that it would hurt anyone all that much, to, at the first of this lecture, say, "Look, we're the Creative Community Project. A lot of us happen to be members of the Unification Church." It's very simple to say that. If you did, then people like Chris Edwards wouldn't be able to make the justifiable claim that he didn't know for three days. That's his major argument, though in fact he did know beforehand.

Richard Quebedeaux: Just think about what it's like to identify yourself as a Moonie in this society . . .

Lewis Rambo: Well, I think that's tough, but I think that's the case with most religious groups.

Richard Quebedeaux: Not any more. No, religion's very popular now. It's in. You can go witness, get born again, give someone the four spiritual laws, and it's sort of chic. When I was an undergraduate at U.C.L.A., Campus Crusade did exactly the same sort of deception. I think we all need to be honest, but I suppose the ethic always comes about that somehow the ends justify the means. Somehow we believe that if we are up-front at first nobody will come because of all the bad press we have in the media, but if they just come there they will know better. They will really understand things.

I understand that. I put together these conferences, and, boy, I'm beginning to wonder—I know what's going to happen when people come. I'm trying to think up the best ways to get people to come . . .

Lewis Rambo: I talked with some people who went to the CARP meeting here recently. Half of the people there were people who were studying the movement. The other half of them, it was my impression, were people who were in one way or another marginal professor types in the Bay Area. By marginal I'm just describing their situation; I don't mean it as a put-down. For example, I mean someone who is a professor of chemistry and a recent immigrant. Well, they get there, and they don't know that CARP is connected with the Unification Church. Of course, I knew before, because of Mike's invitation. I met one guy who was a recent convert to an evangelical church and he didn't know. He just knew that there were some very nice people who insisted, who called him five times. When he discovered the connection, his initial response was to be offended. Now, is he better off having come only to be offended, or not come at all? My impression is frankly, that it would have been better for him not to have come at all. My own opinion is that if one is deceived in a situation like that the tendency would be to discount the movement immediately. And so, I'm bewildered as to why on a simple matter like this you aren't more direct. It is, at least, a safeguard for yourselves.

Mose Durst: I think it is a matter of judgment. I know CARP in all their literature talks about Rev. Moon. And CARP is inviting this professor...

Lewis Rambo: No, he was called on the telephone. He never received any literature.

Mose Durst: He never got any literature?

Lewis Rambo: That was what he told me.

Mose Durst: Our policy, again, is to give out literature to the people CARP invite. On the literature CARP gives a background of their inspiration by Rev. Moon. It's a very analogous situation. It's a question, I think, of judgment. The person comes to a seminar, and signs a form saying, "This seminar is co-sponsored by the Unification Church, or associated with the Unification Church." He's involving himself for a day or two and he knows that if he signs this registration form that that's what he's getting involved with. In my judgment, that's a really clear indication that it was out-front and straight-forward.

Lewis Rambo: I wasn't talking about that. I was talking about the evening session, where it could have been a group of very happy ex-University of California at Berkeley students living in a commune.

Mose Durst: But look at the realism of that. What would...

Lewis Rambo: But it happens to be a lie. That's not what it is.

Mose Durst: That's unfair. If people ask, "What is this," they are told it's the Creative Community Project in association with the Unification Church or CARP or whatever. This is our policy.

Holly Sherman: When I first met the Church and was invited to come over to dinner, I didn't know anything about it but I went. "Out-front" means to me that what they believed was absolutely visible. And it was. I saw seventy or eighty people of all races, nationalities, and backgrounds that really cared about one another sincerely. And even though they didn't know me, they cared sincerely about me. To me, that's being "out-front." They were out-front with what they really believed sincerely. It is there in their life. I never have seen that change in the whole time I've been in the Church. So to me, "out-front" is putting into practice what they really believe.

Lewis Rambo: Yes, and I would agree with that. But I guess it strikes me as just peculiar. . . .

Holly Sherman: Because of what I saw and experienced I became very curious. I thought, "How come this exists? How can this be possible?" And so, I wanted to come and listen to lectures and learn about the doctrine and theology and things like that. In one sense, the doctrine is secondary. What is important was what I saw. What I saw first was what actually was being put into practice!

Lewis Rambo: Well, you see, I'm struck by another group I've been studying, the "Jews for Jesus." They are totally out-front. There's no surprise. They wear T-shirts that sock you in the nose. Here they are in the Los Angeles airport, wearing these big "Jews for Jesus" T-shirts. And there's nothing hidden. It gets them into a lot of trouble. They're offensive to a lot of people. But no one can walk down through the airport and start reading a brochure and say, "Aha! I've been deceived." It's out-front. Everybody knows. There's no surprise.

Holly Sherman: I just don't see how our practice is "deception." I never felt deceived later when I found out what was being taught, because it all went along with what I had seen in the first place. I'd feel deceived if I found out later that actually what they believed was that we should be prejudiced and that we should hate and just live for ourselves. Then I would see deception, but I don't see . . .

Lewis Rambo: Now that's the kind of thing I'm perplexed with. I'm affirmative of the life-style I see. But why is it necessary for you to be hidden and deceptive about who you are? I believe that any truly religious group holds that the ends do not justify the means. Period. And any group that starts talking like that has started violating basic principles. Of course, with honesty, you may have to pay a price. You may not be popular. You may have problems. I admire the Jews for Jesus, because they don't pretend to be anything other than what they are. Anybody who takes a brochure knows exactly what they are getting. It seems to me to be a very simple thing.

Mose Durst: Again, we may be making a mountain out of a molehill. Somebody can come over for dinner, or somebody can come over during the day for tea or coffee, because if you meet somebody, you invite them over to your home. And our centers are our homes. Now this is one thing. But anyone who has any involvement in our programs, who is involved in any formal way, they will do so under the clear knowledge that this is associated with the Unification Church. Any involvement, any commitment whatsoever, whether it be contractual involving payment of money or a commitment of time or of going somewhere for a formal seminar or something, there is a clear indication that this is the Unification Church. I invite people over for coffee. I invite people over for tea. I just may want to talk to someone and see where they are at. They may be completely hostile to the Church, and they say, "Thank you, it's nice having coffee with you, have a good day." I want to see where people are at. We invite strangers into our home every night. It's important for us to see what people want with their lives before we offer them what we have. So we don't offer them the product until we know that they are in the market for that product. When they are in the market, we tell them exactly what the product is, and it's true and honest, and there's no deception. But it's a matter of judgment and distinction when you invite somebody over to your home. I'm talking from real experience of saying to somebody at three in the afternoon, "Why don't we go home for coffee? Let's sit down and chat." And if I see the person is open, I say, "Why don't you stay awhile for the lecture?"

Lewis Rambo: Now, I have no problems with that. But I was there for about three and a half hours. You say the whole thrust of your life is being devoted to God, that your relationship to God is *the* central driving force of your entire existence, and yet I didn't hear God mentioned once. Now that is curious. Why do you do it that way?

Virginia Hearn: I just want to make a passing comment that, since the days that Holly entered the Church, there has been a very bad press. And so, because of that, it's better that you be up-front because people do have those negative associations.

Durwood Foster: Perhaps the point I was going to make has already been sufficiently made. I'm sort of stewing over the issue that does seem to exist here, because it seems to me to be a very universal kind of ethical issue. I think it is a very real issue. I'm not sure that the Unification Church has been egregiously guilty on this score, but I've been trying to define precisely what the problem is. It seems to me that at a microscopic level, in a very miniscule way, the problem already exists in the approach which Dr. Durst engagingly described. That is, when you are at a bus stop with someone, you talk about Mickey Mantle for a bit. However, your real motive in being out there is to witness to God and the Church, but you don't let that be known immediately. You establish a human contact by some kind of humor or human empathy and so on. Is that deceptive already in that very small moment? Because it seems to me that the weekends are simply those kinds of moments enlarged, if you will. It may be that the greater magnitude of the weekend introduces a qualitative difference, I don't know. Magnitude seems to be important to Lewis in that he wouldn't mind if only 15 minutes went by and God wasn't mentioned, but if three and a half hours go by, then he does mind.

Lewis Rambo: It just strikes me as odd.

Durwood Foster: Right. But I wanted to mention some analogous kinds of situations that come to mind as I think about this. The pastor of my one-time Methodist church here in Berkeley, I remember, explained to some of us, on a weekend at a church retreat, his evangelical technique. He'd been rather successful in building up his congregation. He's not evangelical particularly, but he's a very engaging kind of person who's effective in building the church. He said he never comes on in a heavy religious way. He comes on in terms of relating to people humanly, and asking about their families, getting acquainted on that level. He gets to be friends with them. Pretty soon they are coming to church to visit, or whatever, and this winds up with their affiliating with the church. Now, there were some questions raised, when he presented that, about whether this was a good Christian strategy, as there were some who felt he ought to be more theological sooner—whereas this person wasn't particularly theological at all. But I don't think anyone really raised the question of deception. Here was this large group of Methodists sitting around, and no one raised the question. But it seems to me that it *was* in the same way deceptive. If Dr. Durst's procedure is deceptive, then that was at least in some measure similarly deceptive.

Another kind of example that I encountered fairly recently is that I'm right now doing some fund-raising for a national organization to which I belong. It's essentially composed of people who teach in colleges and universities throughout the country, and it's a highly ethically conscious group. It's comprised of people who are teaching philosophy, ethics, theology, literature and so on. When we were being orientated as to how to go about fund-raising—it's critical for the survival of the organization—we were instructed to call the people whom we were to contact and say we wanted to make an appointment with them. But we were not to tell them we wanted to make a pitch to get a pledge from them. As I recall, one or two persons did wonder if that was completely ethical, but we were reassured that this was the way fund-raising was done; and the very great majority in that highly conscientious group did not raise any question about it. And that has been the way in which the fund-raising has been proceeding. We can all think of other kinds of examples, and I must confess that I don't know how to resolve this issue. It is a kind of dilemma, but it runs very pervasively through our lives.

One final illustration, there was a Bob Hope-Bing Crosby movie about 30 years ago that took this theme and played with it. One of them, I think it was Bob Hope, played this role where he was on a "complete candor" kick. He was totally up-front at every moment. The result was that relationships collapsed. It was obviously a kind of farce, but it drew upon the point that in human relations, you simply can't be totally up-front. You don't walk up to a lady on the bus and say, "I think you're really ugly." You smile, and do things that could be called "heavenly deception" because it's for the sake of *agape,* not offending people gratuitously.

Walter Hearn: I have a contrast to offer. In the evangelical circles in which I travel, I'm often concerned about a kind of up-front style some Christians have. It's a style in which one says the right words and lets the chips fall where they may. Some evangelicals want to say certain theological things in order to speak about Jesus Christ, and they have a style of doing it that may repel people. But their concern is to say it, and thus to honor

Christ. I'm concerned about that. Most of the time I would like for them to have some of the spirit that Mose Durst has that says, "Well, what we're really concerned about is reaching this person. But we don't have to say 'Jesus Christ.' We can first say, 'Mickey Mantle'." A little subtlety—and not only subtlety, but the idea of putting the other person's genuine needs first—is needed. That means taking responsibility to step in and serve them in the best way, not just the way that will make you feel better because you've said Christ's name.

But now I want to turn this around because I think Ginny and I are a little concerned about how up-front you are. It seems to me that several questions have been asked to which we, as Christians, would have expected some of you to say something about Jesus Christ in your answers. But you haven't. Rather, you said something about Rev. Moon or about the Church or about an ideal or a loving community or a program, and we find that a cause for concern. Maybe you *are* being up-front. If you are, we're a little concerned. You already know where we stand, I think. I'm sort of surprised that I haven't heard more of Jesus Christ in our conversation when we've been speaking to each other as closely as we can, as brothers and sisters in Christ. I hope you're *not* being up-front. That is, I hope that it's just your style. We have to nail you to the wall and say, "Come on. What is it that really motivates you?" And you would say, "Well, it's Jesus Christ."

Jonathan Wells: I think I've heard Jesus Christ mentioned as much by Unificationists as by evangelicals. (laughter)

Walter Hearn: I would say that it's at critical junctures when questions were asked like "What is the Gospel?" or "What do you say to somebody in need?" that I missed it.

Jonathan Wells: OK. I don't think that's a question of deception. I think that's a question of whether we're heretics or not. (laughter) To get back to the ethical question, it's a valid question, and it's a very important one, but the point that Durwood made is that it's difficult to fix the line where you have to make this ethical stand. And I have just a short story about an incident that happened to me in the dining hall of a famous New England divinity school. One day I was eating lunch and I got to talking to the fellow next to me. Since I was new there, I was meeting everybody for the first time. As we got to talking, I said, "My name is Jonathan Wells." He was from Cuba, and we began to talk about Cuba, communism, and social action; and about ten minutes into the conversation a girl walked over who had recently found out that I was a Moonie. She said, "Oh, Jon, are you still in the Unification Church?" By the tone of her voice, it was evident that she was doing it to be nasty. That wasn't what shocked me. The guy I was talking to jumped out of his chair, started accusing me of deceiving him. I felt I was expected to wear a star like a star of David on my sleeve. It is getting totally ludicrous when I can't even talk to somebody without saying "Hi, I'm Jonathan Wells, from the Unification Church."

Anthony Guerra: I've been wanting to say something for the longest time, and that is this. I think the question of deception has to turn on this focus: whether or not we are saying things which in fact misrepresent what we actually believe, and hence leading people to make certain commitments or contributions on a false basis. And I think that's precisely what's not happening here! Someone comes to a meeting for three hours, and hears this talk about our ethical concerns, but doesn't hear about our doctrine of God or Jesus. I don't see the problem. The person goes away, and he has two options at that point. He can maybe take the advice and start loving people more or forget it. I've taught many groups. If that happens I'm really happy. If a person wants to hear more, then I'm also happy to teach more. But I concede that the mission of building the Kingdom has both very comprehensive and particular focuses, as Dr. Durst was saying. So you give as much as you can when you can. What's being given in a three-hour session when God or Jesus or Rev. Moon is not mentioned is not false. It speaks to one aspect of our commitment, and that's communicated. No one is asked to make a commitment to join the Church or dedicate themselves to the movement at that point.

Lewis Rambo: If the central motivating factor in your life is serving God through Jesus Christ then I can't imagine spending three hours talking without the central motivating factor of your life ever being mentioned. I would question whether that was really the central motivating factor of your life.

Darrol Bryant: I've talked to many people for many hours without. . .

Lewis Rambo: But if in fact you are reaching out, it just strikes me as peculiar that you don't mention. . .

Mose Durst: I don't understand what is so peculiar. . .

Lewis Rambo: Just a second. I'm in a double bind here, because I'm wanting to say to people, "Look, the Unification Church is doing some good things. The people I know in the movement are really fantastic. I know Mike Mickler, I know Mr. Masuda, etc. etc. Now I've met Dr. Durst. They are doing some valuable things." But then they start saying, "Well, I had a friend who went down to such and such, and they never mentioned the Church." Now, what rationale do I give them?

Anthony Guerra: The point is we're taking the mission absolutely seriously to serve God and to serve humanity.

Lewis Rambo: But what are your ultimate goals? What is the really crucial thing for you, for every single human being on the face of the earth? For me, as an evangelical Christian, the ultimate issue is Jesus Christ.

Jonathan Wells: And the ultimate issue for us is the Kingdom of God on earth. And one way to establish it is to raise the ethical standard, raise people's sense of idealism.

Richard Quebedeaux: The last thing I want to hear in a bunch of religious people is about Jesus Christ. I've heard about Jesus Christ in Sunday school since I've been a kid. I want to see Jesus Christ *lived out.* When I see that, I'm going to know something. Then you can talk to me about Jesus Christ and I'll listen to you. For me, "Your actions speak so loudly I can't hear a word you're saying." That's my gut level reaction to what you're saying. I don't know how many groups of evangelicals there are that you can go to and they are always saying "Praise the Lord! Jesus saved me, dah-da-dah."

Darrol Bryant: We will clearly have to continue this discussion but we will have to do it in a different format. I know that there are a couple of people who have said that they absolutely have to leave by 9:30 and I promised that we would formally adjourn at 9:00. It is after 9:00 now, so let me adjourn and then the conversation can continue.

Let me thank all of you very, very much for your participation in this conference. Each of these conferences is unique unto itself but this conference has been especially noteworthy in the sense that it has been one of the most sophisticated and theologically substantial conferences that I have had the occasion to be in over the past two and a half years. And I want to thank all of you who have come and have made that possible.